Chuck Wa

D1052099

Chuck

Wagon Cookin'

Stella Hughes

Illustrated by the author

THE UNIVERSITY OF ARIZONA PRESS
Tucson, Arizona

About the Author

STELLA HUGHES knows real, live chuck wagon cooks, their cowboy clientele, and the skills and appetites that formed this unique partnership. Her more than three decades of ranch life have included Stella's own mastery of the dutch oven, and personally preparing barbecues for up to 2,500 people. An Oklahoma native who dreamed of being a cowgirl, Stella moved with her family to California where her father became a horse and mule commissioner, and she learned trick riding and roped in steer-stopping events at Salinas, Bakersfield, and Los Angeles. Wife of Mack Hughes, long-time manager of the IDT herd on the Apache Reservation, she says, "I ate my first dried apple pie under the Tonto Rim in 1931." Later, having become a convinced Arizonan, she became a member of the Cowbelles, a group devoted to the preservation of Arizona history.

THE UNIVERSITY OF ARIZONA PRESS

Sixth printing 1991

ISBN 0-8165-0432-6
LC No. 74-78567

For the
Arizona State Cowbelles
and especially
Lucille Stone of Mesa,
Dot Tipton of Pomerene,
and
the late Pat Stevenson of Red Rock

Contents

Indexed List of Recipes

Where This Book Came From

WHEN I WAS JUST A PIG-TAILED PRETEENAGER it used to irk me to read a "western" story where the author merely described a meal turned out by the roundup cook as "sumptuous" or "larupin'" or "pot lickin' good." Or to read a vague account of a pioneer family "preserving and drying" food to carry in their covered wagons when crossing the plains. What did the chuck wagon cook cook? What kind of food did the pioneers preserve and dry? I was a long time in finding out.

I was born on a dry farm on the South Canadian River in Oklahoma and lived there the first ten years of my life. My mother was a rabid gardener and a prodigious canner and preserver of food. I might have learned a lot from her if I'd not been so set on being a cowgirl. At that time I was sure cowgirls didn't have to cook — was I ever wrong! I thought all they did was ride a prancing pinto pony, help drive some gentle cattle, twirl a rope and ride off into the sunset with a handsome cowboy — Hoot Gibson, Ken Maynard, and Tom Mix being my models.

The summer I was eleven we moved to California. My father, L. A. Cox, became well known as a horse and mule commissioner where we had spacious yards and an auction barn on Bandini Boulevard just across the river from the Los Angeles stockyards at Vernon. I may not have become a cowgirl but during the next twelve years I certainly became a diversified horsewoman. I learned to trick ride (not very well) and roman ride (standing on two running horses). I showed stockhorses in reining classes at horse shows from Santa Barbara to San Diego and over into Imperial Valley. I learned to drive trotting horses to sulkies and to ride in relay races at rodeos. I even learned to rope and participated in Cowgirls' Steer-Stopping at rodeos in Salinas, Bakersfield, and Los Angeles stockyards in the 1930s. This contest was a timed event where the roper started behind the barrier and the steer was given a twenty-foot score. The cowgirl only had to rope the animal and bring it to a stop facing the roper with the rope taut. The prize money was usually a hundred dollars put up by the rodeo pro-ducers and split fifty, thirty, and twenty to the three fastest times. I didn't get rich on prize money, but what little skill I picked up in the art of roping came in mighty handy over the years in helping on the ranch.

In the summer of 1931 I made my first extended visit to Ari-zona and spent several weeks under the rim of Zane Grey's fabulous Tonto Basin. Here I ate my first dried apple pie, sweetened with wild honey, with a rich flaky crust made from rendered bear fat. It was pure ambrosia . . . no, it wasn't. It was the best derned pie I ever ate.

Even at that early age I was hooked on old-timey ways of cooking, but most of all I was hooked on Arizona. I began at once gathering recipes of dutch oven cookery, tales of cowcamp cooks, food lore, and home remedies for any ailment under the sun.

In 1938 I married Mack Hughes, a real dyed-in-the-wool cow-boy (it took me several years and repeated trips to Arizona to find just the right one), and I became a part of the wonderful ranch life I was so interested in. My education in ranch cooking began in earnest. Wow, did it! Our first year of married life was spent on the edge of the Navajo Reservation on a cow outfit with *me* the cook. Never before has a greenhorn gone through such trial by fire. On roundups there were dust storms, alkali water (or none at all), unsuitable wood (or none at all), heat, flies, and the everlasting wind. In that part of northern Arizona the wind blows thirteen months out of the year. Twelve months of that time it blows real hard. The ranch house was a barnlike affair where you could see the sky through the roof and the ground through the floor. No running water (the windmill was a hundred yards away), no ice box, and if there had been there was no ice to put in it. The cook stove was an old worn-out wood-burning monster with the ridic-ulous name of Southern Comfort. The nearest town was a twisting, rutted thirty-five miles away.

Besides all these obstacles, the ranch owner was very stingy with grub. His idea of a well-stocked larder was a slab of salt-crusted half-rancid sowbelly, pinto beans, and canned green chili.

When Mack and I moved to the Apache Indian Reservation we lived at a stockmen's station seventy-five rough miles from San Carlos, the nearest village. Here I entered the College of Dutch Oven Cookery. The Apaches were then, and some still are, adept at cooking with hardwood coals, and I learned a great deal from them.

Over the years Mack has hired scores of Mexican horse-breakers. These good friends from south of the border taught me how to barbecue the "deep pit" style — everything from a quarter of beef to stuffed Thanksgiving turkey to pots of frijoles. My knowledge of barbecuing was put to the supreme test in 1972 when the Apache Tribe hired me to feed 2,500 people at a meeting to vote on a land deal. Mack and I, our son Skeeter, and two others cut, wrapped, and barbecued 1,600 pounds of fine beef. Since then I've been asked to "put on" several other "feeds." But I really don't like to cook! I'd still rather be a cowgirl.

Each year when Mack trailed a herd of cattle, averaging 1,400 head, on a five or six day drive to market, I always went along, but certainly not as cook. Oh, I was on standby in case the cook quit (and they nearly always do before the cattle are shipped), but I drove cattle all the way and said fervent prayers each day that the cook stayed until the drive was over. Truly there is no harder job than slinging heavy dutch ovens and preparing meals for eighteen to twenty men over an open fire.

I've cooked over a lot of fires for a lot of cowboys — and I've talked to old-timers who wandered in the mysteries of chuck wagon cooking all their lives. What I've learned from the old cooks and from necessity is in this book.

STELLA HUGHES

PART I

Recollections

STELLA HUGHES—ARIZONA

Only a damned fool would argue with a skunk,
a woman, or a roundup cook.

Kitchen on Wheels

THE FIRST REAL CHUCK WAGON did not materialize overnight. However, the evolution of the chuck wagon, as we know it today, took only a very brief span of years. The first cow-hunting crowds were a conglomeration of ranchers and farmers — large and small — and each brought his own provisions, either tucked inside his bedroll or hung over the back of the saddle in traps or a wallet. Before the Civil War some of the more prosperous brought a Negro slave to "do" for them, otherwise each man did his own cooking which consisted of the most simple fare. Beef was killed when needed and shared by all. Sometimes the grub was pooled and one or two elected to do the cooking.

Later, when cattle became a more profitable business, there was a little more organization. A cook was hired and grub was packed on mules in regular pack saddles, with kyacks and panniers for carrying the cooking utensils and provisions. When working the treeless plains, ox-drawn carts were used. These were topheavy affairs, but could be drawn over the trailless prairie by a double yoke of oxen. The use of carts and pack mules, though simple, served well as long as the cow work went on near "home," and fresh supplies could be had on fairly short notice.

Probably the first real chuck wagon was taken "up the trail" in 1866, on what was possibly the first large cattle drive to the railroad.

Oliver Loving and Charles Goodnight, Texas partners, drove a herd of two thousand head of mixed stuff — cows, steers and bulls — over the Horsehead Route. The very first chuck wagon was

[7]

used on this trip. Made to Goodnight's specifications, the vehicle was a large, four-wheeled affair, with bows and covered over with waterproof wagon sheets. Below the wagon was slung a device known as a "cooney" or "caboose." In some parts of the country it was called a "coosie" or "possum belly." It was a green cowhide, fastened under the wagon by its corners. In this handy storage area could be carried dry wood or cow chips, when traversing the "bald plains." A jockey box in front was used for storing the simple tools needed on the trail, such as hammers, horseshoe nails, or ax handles. In the rear a tall box was fitted to the exact width of the wagon, with a stout lid that lowered to serve as a work table. This box contained shelves and drawers to hold food and utensils. Under this chuck box some built a rack with a lid for storing the heavy dutch ovens, fire irons, coffee pot, and frying pans.

Besides provisions, the big wagon carried shovels, axes, coils of extra rope, the bedrolls of the cowboys, and any personal belonging they might consider necessary to take along. With space at a high premium it would have to be a very important item, indeed, to warrant hauling the great distances traveled. A banjo or fiddle would be considered essential if one of the men could play it.

Goodnight's first wagon was drawn by ten yoke of oxen, but soon after, the oxen were abandoned for teams of light horses or mules. Other refinements found their way in the form of water barrels with outside spigots, coffee mills bolted to the chuck box, and waterproof flies attached to the back of the wagon as protection from the elements.

This carryall then became the early trail driver's "home-away-from-home," and after the cattle drives came to an end, the cattle ranchers used chuck wagons for working their vast ranges — sometimes having a "wagon" going as long as four or five months out of a year.

A large outfit with as many as fifteen men and several "reps" or "stray men" from neighboring outfits often outfitted a second wagon, called the "hoodlum wagon" or "bed wagon," and in it was carried bedding, tents, and any supplies spilled over from the chuck wagon.

Nearly always in the northern states, a cook tent or fly was provided for the chuck wagon. The tent was large enough for the wagon to be backed into far enough to cover the chuck box and

worktable. With an arrangement such as this, the cook usually had a small cast iron stove set up in the tent.

In the dry Southwest such comforts as tents and stoves were seldom seen. A waterproof fly attached to the back of the wagon and stretched over the cook's work area was considered sufficient.

This is where the old-time cowcamp cook came into his own. There was no particular kind of camp cook. They ran the gamut from Negro to "Portugee," Mexican or Chinese; however, most were white and generally middle-aged or older men, as young men were not considered capable of taking on such a task. Cooking over a campfire for a number of men was an art and not learned overnight.

A good roundup cook was a wondrous and versatile man. There wasn't anything he couldn't cook under almost insurmountable difficulties — from lack of proper firewood (oak, mesquite, any hardwoods) to minor incidents like stampedes, blizzards, dust storms, floods, and rattlesnakes.

He was an expert at scrounging and improvising when the chuck ran low, and could "make do" as long as the coffee didn't run out and he had flour. The mainstay of the range diet, then as well as now, was beef, and that was always at hand. All meals were built around some form of beef, and variations depended on the skills of the cook and local customs.

The old time cowboy cook ruled his chuck wagon and cooking area with an iron hand. There were unwritten laws no self-respecting cowboy would dream of violating. Riding into camp, the cowboy *always* stayed downwind. Woe betide the unfortunate rider who dashed by stirring up a cloud of dust. There were camp rules of etiquette that only a greenhorn would voluntarily break. Crowding around the cook's fire for warmth was a taboo that was almost never broken. The space between the fire and chuck box was sacrosanct, and belonged to the cook and he alone. Cowboys provided separate wood and warming fires for themselves while the cook was at work. These fires were referred to as "bull" fires, and pitch and other unsuitable wood for cooking was used. Never did they use the oak, mesquite, or other hardwoods so necessary for dutch oven cooking. Nor could any cowboy walk into camp and help himself to a snack, or even a cup of coffee, until invited to do so by the cook.

After finishing a meal, the cowboys scraped their plates clean and put them in a tub or pan provided by the cook. This receptacle was often referred to as the "wrecking barrel." Any unfortunate cow-waddy that left a cup, plate, or knife lying around might find himself on the short end of the cook's serving spoon next meal.

No horses were left tethered or hobbled near the chuck wagon, regardless how many "Westerns" or T.V. movies might show one practically drooling down the cook's neck. Nor was a cowboy's bedroll or personal belongings strewn near "Cookie's" domain, where they could be stumbled over.

If the cook didn't have a flunky, or the horse wrangler was unable to help, the cowboys themselves snaked in firewood at the end of saddle ropes for camp. Cowboys who were not immediately needed elsewhere when breaking camp, fell to and hitched the horses to the wagon and loaded supplies and bedrolls with a cheerful mien.

Keeping the "Cookie" happy paid off in wonderful dividends. Although not a gourmet, the cowboy liked good food. If an army travels on its stomach, roundups were a success or a failure depending on the skill of the cook and the largess of the outfit employing him. A stingy owner who tried to cut operating costs at the expense of the cowboy's stomach found himself short of hands come roundup time.

Albert Hawley, at one time Superintendent of the White River Apache Indian Reservation, often ate at the various roundup camps. He swore the success of a roundup depended entirely on a good cook and a competent horse wrangler. For what cowboy could be expected to do a hard day's work on an empty stomach, riding a gaunt horse?

A man who made cooking his business drew higher wages than anyone except the boss. In trail driving days, a cook, be he Anglo, Negro, Chinese, or Mexican, might receive sixty dollars a month, while regular cowboys drew only thirty dollars. The typical cowboy was a fair cook but would deem it an insult if asked to cook for a bunch of his fellow workers — unless in case of an emergency — and then he would consider the chore only temporary and feel he was merely "helping out."

The cook got up earlier than anybody else — usually about three o'clock — and had to work longer hours. A good cook would always plan ahead and when moving camp would cook the night before — pans of roast meat, a big pot of beans, along with extra bread so that at no time would he be caught short and any cowboy have to go hungry.

Down through the history of the cattle industry comes the traditional belief that cowcamp cooks were temperamental and cantankerous. Some of the cook's crankiness was based on his desire to keep his camp clean and in order — something like when a mother has a screaming fit when the kids track mud on the freshly mopped kitchen floor — simple as that.

J. Frank Dobie, who lived in Live Oak County, Texas, said the old-time cowcamp cooks were the most even-tempered men he ever knew — mad all the time! Be that as it may, anyone who has ever spent one hour over a campfire on a windy day, or wet — who has burned his thumb, spilled the coffee, scorched the beans, found blowflies have gotten to the meat, and the water keg empty, will understand why cooks are "tetchy."

Lucille Stone, of Mesa, Arizona, tells of a cook she once knew, who after burning the bread, went out and shot himself. The fact this poor man had a history of mental unrest had nothing to do with it.

When Alfred Haught, a lifelong rancher from Young, Arizona, heard I was writing a book on chuck wagon cooks, he endorsed the idea with enthusiasm.

"There's just one thing I want to know," he told me earnestly. "Seein' as you're writin' a book you must be an expert on roundup cooks. Now, tell me, why in hell the owners of cow outfits always hired the meanest, crankiest cooks in the world?"

Well, first of all I don't pretend to be an expert on roundup cooks and fortunately I didn't have to answer Alfred's question, for R. M. Grantham, Alfred's neighbor in Gila County, had the answer to that one. The resulting discussion was summed up this way.

The owners of the cow outfits didn't hire mean cranky cooks a-tall. They merely hired ordinary men that said they could cook. If they turned out to be nasty-tempered, irritable, petulant, always on the prod and "tetchy" as hell, it was all due to the nature of their job.

A man might be the sweetest dispositioned human that ever walked the face of the earth; he could be kind and benevolent, mild-tempered, good-natured, amiable and placid, but just let him hire out as a cook for some roundup and his character would change as drastically as Dr. Jekyll and Mr. Hyde. Overnight he would become an antisocial cowboy hater, a wife beater, and a dog kicker, dishing out meals under an atmosphere as gloomy as a wake. Bilious of eye and caustic of tongue, he hated everybody, most of all himself.

Now, it stands to reason this description couldn't possibly fit all camp cooks, but most that ate at Bill Woods' wagon could agree at least half these adjectives fit Ole Bill to a T. One story concerning his actions (and words) in defending his rights and sanctity of the cook's tent, happened when Woods was cooking for the Pitchforks in Northern Arizona back in the twenties.

The Pitchforks was one of the few outfits that provided the comforts of a large tent which served as both kitchen and dining room. Here the cook reigned supreme, and no monarch could have demanded more of his serfs than did Bill Woods of the cowboys. Bent from arthritis or from stooping over his ovens, he ruled his domain arrogantly. The cowboys had to do the dishes, haul the water, chop and pack the wood, and woe betide the unfortunate one that brought in wood not the proper length for the huge range.

Some considered Bill a good cook and others said only fair, but all agreed he was the crankiest man alive, bar none. Ed Hardt, in telling of the cook's nasty disposition, shook his head in wonder. "He was so cantankerous a shepherd dog couldn't get along with him," he was heard to remark on one occasion.

Sam Simmons, better known as Gallopin' Sam, was repping for the U Bars that fall. He was a good cowboy and well liked, but the mildest thing that could be said about his character was that he was "wilder than hell." Sam also had his own peculiar ideas on how to get along with "bowed up" or "proddy" cooks.

Returning to camp one evening, one of the cowboys dared Sam to ride his horse into the cook's tent. No sooner said than done. Sam set spurs to old "Straight Edge," a U Bar horse only a little less wild than his rider, and with a squall that could be heard a mile, charged through the tent flaps. He was about half inside when Bill Woods threw a butcher knife. The sharp blade stuck in the upright of the tent only inches from Gallopin' Sam's head. It changed his mind.

The wrathy cook followed Sam outside, cussing and yelling. Later, those telling of the cook's tirade, did so in awe. Never before, or since, had the cowboys heard so much unprintable profanity, and not one of them was a slouch when it came to cussing.

Keelo Pruitt, the wagon boss, later remarked, "That old cook really scorched Sam's hide like a cracklin'. You could even smell the fat a-burnin'. The incident didn't improve the cook's disposition none either," Pruitt concluded.

As for Gallopin' Sam, he cackled in glee and turned his horse in the remuda and returned to "rawhide" the cook and cajole him back into his usual humor, which was just short of the knife-throwing stage.

We live on jerky gravy
And soggy sourdough bread.
Coffee strong as alkali,
It's a wonder we ain't dead.

What the Eatin' Was

NOT ALL ROUNDUP COOKS were good cooks, nor did all owners provide ample supplies. One ranch down in the southern part of Arizona — best left unnamed — was more than skimpy on chuck, and was known from Canada to the Mexican border as the "Macaroni Cattle Company." Some cowboys working for this outfit swore they were lucky if they got the "tomaters" to go with the macaroni.

Eggs were seldom found in a chuck box. Those few the cook could scrounge from the hen house at the home ranch were hoarded like gold, and used in cakes and puddings. No cowboy expected ham and eggs for breakfast. Large juicy steaks, pan gravy, and sourdough biscuits were the kind of breakfast that stuck to a man's ribs, and just might tide him over until night. Sometimes there was a dutch oven of fried potatoes. "Mush" or oatmeal was cooked and served with canned milk — when they had the milk. Most outfits supplied plenty of bacon and salt pork, as it kept well and could be used in everything. However, beef was handy and plentiful and was served at every meal, day in and day out.

Fresh vegetables were as scarce as eggs, and with thousands of cows on the range, fresh milk wasn't even thought of. Potatoes and onions were the only perishable vegetables found in a chuck wagon. Most outfits even held canned goods to a minimum with canned corn — cream style — heading the list, and canned tomatoes — being a most versatile commodity — nearly always in plentiful supply. Few bought canned fruit as it was heavy to pack and expensive. The early-day cooks thought dried or evaporated fruit superior anyhow. Dried apples were the most popular — with peaches and apricots, prunes and raisins being used by most cooks.

A box of cinnamon, a bottle of vanilla, and salt and pepper were the only seasonings necessary, and with these any cook worth his wages could prepare meals fit for a king.

If chuck boxes were shy of eggs, butter, fresh milk, seldom saw a fresh vegetable, and only canned or dehydrated fruit, a person might wonder with some concern, "What in the world did they eat?" Now, don't fret. When a cow outfit had a cook worth his salt, they ate, and ate well. No one could complain after dining on a T-bone steak that had been cut from a grass-fat yearling, dipped in flour, and fried in a dutch oven — and so tender you could have eaten it without teeth — along with pinto beans, cooked with chunks of salt pork and seasoned to perfection, and a generous serving of Spanish rice, flavored with chilies and tomatoes, and baked in a dutch oven. Back this up with sourdough biscuits, browned to a crusty perfection — no one ever missed the butter — topped off with a huge helping of cobbler made of dried apples or peaches and covered with a flaky pie crust made of pure leaf lard. Then, if you were still hungry, you might make one more trip to the bread oven, and top off that last biscuit with "lick" (syrup), or wild honey.

Nutritionists, upon hearing of this diet, throw up their hands and shudder. All carbohydrates and fats — no eggs, milk, or green, leafy vegetables — horrors! But wait: do not condemn so hastily. Let's face a few facts and ask some honest questions. Did you ever see a fat cowboy? Not in those days you didn't. People subsisting on a diet of principally beef and beans had the whitest and most perfect teeth of anyone. No one had ever heard of cholesterol in the blood, and the only people on ranches that died of heart attacks were old people in their nineties, and even *that* was caused by drinking too much coffee or whiskey.

Any young cowboy that crawled out of his "soogans" two hours before dawn and was ten miles from camp at sunrise, rode, roped, wrestled calves, sweated over a branding fire, and "rode down" two horses before dark, was bound to require energy food and lots of it. So if the diet was beef, beans, biscuits, and more of the same, all we can say is "Thank God!"

You can ask any old-time cowboy if he ever missed the so-necessary fresh fruit and vegetables, or craved something besides beef — chicken, for instance.

"Chicken!" he would snort. Why, chicken was fine eating, but only available when you got sick, or it did. Oranges were for convalescing, and a cowboy might see only one in a year — and that in the bottom of a kid's Christmas stocking handed out at the school doin's.

So, the old-timer — when he had his druthers — simply skipped the vegetables, and partook of extra helpings of beef and potatoes.

Mack Hughes, manager of the San Carlos Apache Tribal Ranch for many years, as a seventeen-year-old worked for an outfit near Ely, Nevada. This was back in 1926, and large and small outfits ran their cattle on open range. At roundup time the home-steaders that farmed along the river would all throw in together. This was known as a "pool," and each owner would provide his share of the chuck. Most of the nesters had gardens and small farm plots, and in the fall vegetables were abundant, with carrots, turnips, squash and cabbage heavy on the market. Also, most of them raised hogs and cured their own salt pork — commonly known as "sow-belly" or "sow bossom." Each owner taking part in the pool brought a wagonload of such truck.

Mack swears to this day he nearly died of starvation. Even after over forty years, he can barely stand the sight or smell of boiled vegetables and sowbelly. The cook, in order to utilize this tremen-dous supply of vegetables, concocted huge pots of boiled salt pork with carrots, turnips, and cabbage, for every meal. Nor did this certain cook make bread or biscuits, but instead served cornbread three times a day, as the nesters had also brought sack after sack of homeground cornmeal. Now there's nothing wrong with corn-bread once in awhile, but anyone used to sourdough bread, biscuits, and pancakes, is going to get mighty tired of straight corn pone.

Mack says only his pride and sense of duty made him stick it out until the roundup was over, and then he left for Arizona as fast as that Model T jitney could run. Back to beef, beans, and bis-cuits — food that would stick to a man's ribs.

Most cowmen did not care for soup, and a bowl of quivering Jello was once passed upon, by an old-timer, as having "about as much sustenance to it as running against the wind with a funnel in your mouth." Which brings up the story as told to me by Bill Lovelady of Winslow, Arizona.

Bill Lovelady's friends called him "Lovey." He ran a few cows up around the Chevelon Butte country — about where the corners of Navajo and Coconino counties meet. Often, on his trips to town, Lovey would visit his friend the Judge, and his wife. The Judge's wife was notorious for her skimpy and frugal board. Anyhow, to hear Lovey tell it, he shied away from the Judge's house at meal-time. But, one day, there was no way of escaping, and Lovey partook of "lunch." It was "dinner" to Lovey, but as it turned out, it wasn't enough fare to satisfy a hummingbird. Lovey later related, in wonder, the menu. A small bowl of clear consommé — "come-sue-me," Lovey called it. He said she had little-bitty pieces of toast, instead of crackers, and tiny sandwiches with the crusts trimmed off, for Christ's sake! There was a minute serving of plain Jello for dessert. Then, to top it off, instead of *hot* coffee, she served glasses of *iced* coffee! Lovey nearly gagged on the cold coffee, as he was used to drinking it scalding hot from a tin cup.

A short while after lunch, Lovey and the Judge went back downtown. Standing on the main street corner, Lovey suddenly blurted out, "Say, Judge, let's go eat." Then he could have crawled into a hole and pulled it after him, he was so overcome with embarrassment. The Judge, however, replied heartily, "Damned good idee," and treated Lovey and himself to steak, mashed potatoes, corn-on-the-cob, biscuits, and apple pie à la mode, at the Harvey House.

Clair Haight, an old-time easy-going Texan, often cooked for the Hashknife outfit in the twenties. Clair probably came close to being truly ingenious as a roundup cook. His sourdough bread was hard to beat, and dutch oven cakes, cobblers, pies, and puddings, are long remembered by anyone lucky enough to have eaten at his wagon.

Clair was adept at preserving and canning, and "putting down" food for long keeping. At his own little homestead, thirty-five miles south of Winslow, Arizona, he had a well-stocked cellar. Here were crocks of homemade butter that kept fresh and sweet for months. He kept eggs in waterglass (sodium silicate or potassium silicate, usually dissolved in water to form a syrupy liquid as a preservative) for as long as a year; and there were shelves groaning from their burden of homemade cheese — and cabbages, wrapped in newspapers, that kept all winter. Pumpkins and winter squash were stored likewise. There were jellies, jams, and preserves — made of everything from prickly pear apples to wild grapes, and currants and wild plums. Tins full of clear, amber honey, gathered from wild bees, sat on the earthen floor. He had jerky made from beef, as well as venison and elk, hanging from rafters in sacks. His home-cured hams and bacon were the best in the country. He put up his own sausage by frying patties and layering them in crocks, and pouring melted lard over them. No woman could beat Clair when it came to making hominy. Clair's hominy was snow white, tender, and flavorsome.

Growing his own corn in a small patch, he also ground his own cornmeal. He used the corn for other things besides meal and hominy. His corn whiskey carried the greatest wallop of any in Navajo County. He didn't have the field to himself either. Competition was stiff — as every rancher had his own moonshine still in those days. Clair was not only talented in distilling strong spirits, but his home brew was the finest ever capped — and his wild grape wine was declared the warmest ever drank. With a larder and cellar as described, it is no wonder all the other bachelors in the country hung out at Clair's little ranch.

Now, anyone reading this would believe Old Clair had a fine piece of rich farmland, irrigated by unlimited supply of water, along with a fine orchard of fruit and nut trees, as well as a variety of berry bushes. Surely a person would visualize his flock of plump Rhode Island Red hens, laying great big brown eggs in a nice lice-free chicken house. And, naturally, with the butter and cheese Clair stored in his cellar, anyone would just *know* he had several Holstein or Jersey milk cows, with great swollen bags just a' dragging the ground, waiting to be milked night and morning.

Well, anyone imagining any such thing would be dead wrong! For Clair's tiny rocky piece of farmland saw water only when it rained, and in that part of northern Arizona it forgot to rain for months at a time.

Clair planted his corn as the Navajo did, in clumps, and if he were lucky would gather a fair crop of Indian corn in the fall. Pinto beans and pumpkins were hardy enough to vie with the rocks and jackrabbits, and Clair could depend on a slim margin of success.

As for fruit, Clair didn't even have an orchard. Fruit trees need water. Clair's water supply was a cistern for house use, and a dirt tank built to catch run-off water for stock. Many years he hauled water in barrels from Chevelon Creek.

Clair made a trip each summer to the Hopi Reservation, where he brought back a wagonload of little red Spanish peaches, apples, pears, and grapes. Wild plums were gathered on the Colorado River, and black walnuts and wild grapes, as well as choke and elderberries on Chevelon Creek.

Clair's flock of laying hens were a motley bunch of half-game that were as wild as quail, and were only a little less trackable than his milk cows. For Clair's milk stock were often straight range cows with maybe a thirty-second of a cross of dairy stock. Each cow — and they changed periodically — had to be necked to a post, side-lined and hobbled, before a man could even begin to think of milking her. Cows of this kind had their advantages, as Clair could turn them out with their calves, and take off on some cooking job for several months with no harm done except, possibly, make Bossy wilder by the respite — if that were possible.

Clair considered his luck phenomenal if he were able to save half of a litter of pigs from the varmints, until they were of butchering size. For, like his poultry, his pigs ran wild and fattened off the vast crop of acorns in the fall.

In those days, Clair had only to go out a short distance to down a fine buck deer or antelope, or bring in a mess of quail or a fat gobbler. When he tired of wild game, Old Clair was even known to butcher one of his own beeves. Something most of his neighbors couldn't brag about.

Of all the gourmet dishes Clair was known for cooking in camp, he probably excelled best at making the cowboy's favorite — son-of-a-bitch stew. In polite circles, or if women were around, it was called son-of-a-gun or simply S.O.B. Sometimes it might be referred to as "Forest Ranger" or "Range Boss," or "County Attorney," or anyone else that might be in disfavor at the time. The possibilities for names were unlimited.

One day at the Hashknife wagon, Clair was busily dicing heart, liver, sweetbreads, kidneys, and guts, in preparation of dinner for a dozen cowboys. One of the men rode into camp early. Viewing Clair's activities, this cowboy beamed, and said, "Well, I see we can expect a son-of-a-bitch for supper." Clair never batted an eye, and replied, "Yep, I expect about twelve of 'em."

Jeff Patterson, when he first came West from Chicago in 1900, said he was somewhat startled when invited to a cannibalistic feast, when visiting his first roundup camp. Said he declined the invitation, with the excuse that he'd known lots of 'em, but never had no intention of eatin' one.

All roundup cooks were not of Clair's caliber, however. Some were awful cooks, and no matter how well-stocked the grub box, they managed to ruin the food in cooking. Some either burned the beans, or served them rattling in the pot — half-cooked. Others either salted too much, or left it out entirely. Some south-of-the-border cooks had a heavy hand with chili and ruined it for those that did not like their food hot and spicy. And so it went — but cooks, at their worst, found it hard to ruin good tender beef. That is, Mack Hughes always thought so until he hired Ole Whiskey.

This was during a roundup of the Ash Creek Association on the San Carlos Reservation. Mack was stockman for this spread in the late forties. Good Apache cooks are few and far between, and at this fall gatherin' Mack was caught with one of the lesser talented ones. Ole Whiskey was good humored and fairly clean, but his cooking left much to be desired. The Apache cowboys are used to eating plain, poorly prepared food — and do not have a reputation for fine cookery. But like anyone else, they enjoy good food. After a week or so of Ole Whiskey's disastrous meals, even they registered a complaint.

For Ole Whiskey boiled meat and served it half done at every meal, including breakfast. He would tackle a quarter of fine beef with his butcherknife and saw off chunks, cutting the meat every-which-way. When he got through the bones looked like coyotes had feasted on the carcass. Never was a bone disjointed or a steak cut. Also, Whiskey's idea of meat done enough to eat was when it had boiled just long enough to turn blue. His beans were so hard they rattled like buckshot in a boxcar.

So, Mack took Ole Whiskey to one side and told him he had better cook the beans a little longer, and thought it might be a good idea to let the flunky cut a few steaks once in a while. Mack dug out the meat saw for them to use. Ole Whiskey took it in good humor, and said, "Okay Mack, I'll see what I can do." After that, there was an occasional meal with fried steaks, but even those were cut with the grain of the meat and almost impossible to eat.

On a trip to town one day, the truck driver and his swamper hijacked the menu from the local cafe. This was a sign painted on a board, about two feet high by five feet in length. On it were listed such items as Hamburgers, Cheeseburgers and French Fries, Rib

Steaks and T-bones, Chicken Fried Steak and Chili and Beans, Ice cream and Pie à la mode. This sign was carried along in the truck, and put up in a prominent place at each camp. It went all through the two month long roundup. It may not have improved the meals any, but the Apaches enjoyed their joke.

Don Thompson, who was a stockman for the Apaches, both on the San Carlos and White River reservations, tells of several cooks he had that had learned their trade working for white outfits off the Reservation. They had learned to bake light-bread and how to make cobblers, and other fixin's foreign to their past way of life — sometimes improvising in strange ways — as Don once found out.

He told of one cook who built a cornstarch pudding, using at least a dozen eggs and cans and cans of milk, and sweetened it with plenty of sugar. It looked just right — not too thick and not too thin, so Don ladled a big helping on his plate. Upon taking the first bite, Don noticed something out of place. Giving the pudding a closer examination, Don discovered the cook had added a can of peas.

The strangest meal anyone ever heard of was a breakfast served by another Apache cook who was hired by the same outfit on another occasion. The roundup was working on the Gila River; and one night the cook walked to a nearby village and joined a tulapai party. Oddly enough, he returned before daylight, weaving unsteadily into camp with a watermelon under each arm. These he managed to slice and serve for breakfast, along with a gallon of string beans, before retiring to his tent to sleep it off. In telling of the incident later, Don slung his head and swore, "Them beans weren't even het up!"

"Tulapai" or "tulpai" is an Apache word and literally means "grey water." "Tu" is water. This volcanic drink is made from fermented corn. It takes several weeks to run off a batch. First, gunny sacks of whole corn are wetted down and kept damp until the corn sprouts. This may take about two weeks. Then the corn is ground, boiled, and reground. Then it is set to ferment — all kinds of native herbs are added. The drink itself might not be so deadly, but what the Apaches add to it to give it "umph" makes it lethal. When the tulapai is ready for consumption they sometimes add a bottle of Levi Garrett's snuff or a plug of Brown Mule chewing tobacco or a sack of Bull Durham. Either or all prove very potent. Many avoid such fireworks and prefer to mix in local herbs.

I drank a dipperful of tulapai once, and it was like sipping dirty, greasy dishwater. Looked like it too. I strained the tobacco grains through gaps in my front teeth. It blew the top of my head off! But, boy, I wouldn't let them know it for one million dollars. Especially after I'd been warned White Eyes couldn't drink it!

Bill Jim Wyrick used to have a ranch a few miles north of Winslow, Arizona, and a forest permit fifty miles south of the Colorado River, where he moved his cattle for the summer months. Each year, when trailing about four hundred head of cows and calves to this summer range, he would hire extra help for the four or five day's drive. He did not hire a cook, but the men took turns, or all fell to and helped prepare the meals.

Bill Jim drove his pickup as the chuck wagon, and the first day out stopped off in town to buy a supply of chuck for the trip. Either he never had a list or lost it, for he ended up in camp that evening shy several important items. He forgot lard, but had purchased two slabs of bacon. So each meal, before meat could be fried or bread made, one of the cowboys sliced and rendered bacon, reserving the grease. Besides forgetting lard, Bill Jim had failed to buy any canned goods at all, except for three cases of spinach. Now, spinach is a fine food, rich in iron and other muscle building vitamins; but I have yet to meet a cowboy that would eat it except under threat of punishment. Bill Jim's crew was far from being an exception.

A beef had been butchered the eve before the drive started, so each meal they had beef and spinach, and spinach and beef. With no canned milk, they made water gravy, and water biscuits. Besides a lot of spinach, they had plenty of fried bacon. Yet, no matter how much bacon was fried before a meal, they never seemed to have enough grease.

There were five men on this drive, and at no time did one ever complain or utter a gripe. The fact Bill Jim was redheaded, and might prove to be a bit "tetchy" on the subject, could have had some bearing on their behavior. So they went right on pretending spinach was high on their list of vegetables suitable for camp fare, and gallantly consumed almost two cases of the stuff before some of them began to toss gobs of it into the brush when they thought Bill Jim wasn't looking.

On the last day of the drive, almost in sight of the ranch, one of Bill Jim's prize bulls laid down and died, right in the middle of the trail. There was a great deal of speculation as to what could have caused the bull's untimely demise. Bill Jim sat on his horse, and worriedly scratched his head in perplexity. Finally, he said, "Must'a been something he et."

One of the cowboys, Lute Smith, considered for a moment, and then asked in studied seriousness, "Bill, you think it likely he might'a ate some of that spinach?"

Just for a moment there was a stunned silence, and then Bill Jim gathered up his reins and chuckling, said, "That would have done it, Lute. That *sure* would have done it." Then he loped on to catch up with the herd.

Here's a menu of a dinner served on a ranch in West Texas in about 1868. This was a festive occasion and considered by the author as "eatin' high on the hog."

Roast venison with brown gravy
Fried catfish (caught from the river that morning)
Squirrel stew
Blackeye peas
Corn-on-the-cob
Cornbread with fresh churned butter
Cold buttermilk
Wild honey
Plum jam
Sliced cucumbers with sour cream
Watermelon rind pickles

This dinner was no doubt in late summer — witness the fresh corn-on-the-cob and fresh cucumbers.

Next is a chuck list ordered from a store in Austin, Texas, in 1878. It's interesting to note whiskey and tobacco head the list. One wonders what the thread was for. Almost certain no woman ordered it or there would have been a choice of color. Probably it was used for sewing on buttons.

1 barl whiskey	1 box Baker Chocolath
2 cast tobaco	55# cone sugar
2 barls flower	1 barl coal-oil
2 barls salt pork	1 gal turpentine

1 barl molasses
4 box dried fruit
50# salt
1 barl lard
5# saleratus
100# corn
1 box spice
200# beans
1 crat Gates matches

1 keg vinegar
2 lantern
2 ax handle
1 shovel
1 coil rope
4 box Arbuckle coffee
20# tea
1 reel wax thread

Sometime before 1863 and until the late 1930s, Arbuckle & Co. were Pittsburgh coffee roasters. They packaged coffee beans in one- and two-pound bags and sold them by the thirty- and fifty-pound crate. These were very sturdy wooden boxes with handholds cut in each end. You can imagine the many uses these boxes were put to in a lumber-shy pioneer West. I've seen kitchen cupboards built entirely from Arbuckle crates. They made fine chairs or camp stools, and no bunkhouse was complete without several nailed to the walls to serve as catchalls. Then they made handy bedside tables to hold the alarm clock and sundry notions, such as Bull Durham and a bottle of Mentholatum. There would be a box under each cot or bunk filled to overflowing with a cowboy's "thirty years gatherin's." Out at the blacksmith shop Arbuckle's boxes contained horseshoes, nails, rivets, and scrap leather. At the chuck wagon the sturdy containers were filled with cups, plates, and "silverware," which the cowboys called "kitchen tools." There would be one box with the medicine supply — concoctions mostly for ailments of horses. The cowboys weren't supposed to get sick.

Along in the 1920s Mack remembers Arbuckle's packed a stick of peppermint candy in each package of their coffee. The Hugheses were so poor that Mack says it was the only candy the kids got between one Christmas stocking and the next.

Chase & Sanborn was the first firm to pack and ship roasted coffee in sealed cans. This was in 1878, and although Chase & Sanborn was a very familiar household term, it must have not caught on with the chuck wagon set. I think it was that nice hefty wooden box that sold the cattle people on Arbuckle's coffee. Then again, it may have been a cheaper brand. At one time Arbuckle's sold for seventeen or eighteen cents a pound.

Beef

Cowboys were, and still are, great beef eaters. The cowman was, and still is, his own best customer, eating meat every day, year in and year out, and meat means *beef*. Whether it was in the form of T-bones, sirloin steaks, ribs, roast or just plain jerky, great quantities of it were consumed on the roundups, and no cowman liked to eat his own beef. He couldn't afford to. He had to butcher his neighbor's in order to keep even. They knew the neighbors ate their stray cattle every chance they got, and this fact was accepted as a rangeland joke.

A cowman, upon setting down to the table of a neighboring rancher would say, "Sure will be a change to eat my own beef." This was always good for a big hearty laugh. Sometimes too hearty. When returning the call, this certain rancher would say, "This beef is mighty tasty, but liable to give me the trots, eatin' my own meat this way, ha-ha-ha-ha-ha-ha-ha."

No one really considered this stealing as long as the person butchering the beef had reason to believe his strays were being consumed in like manner on other ranches. But it was entirely a different story if a person was caught butchering cattle when they themselves owned none. Many a high cottonwood limb has been decorated with the swinging bodies of those that tried this and were caught.

Butchering illegal beef was called "slow elk," and the penalty for such a crime was five years in the penitentiary, if not sudden death by a 30-30 bullet. After ranges became fenced and more settled, there was an end to such practices. But not entirely, for no matter how many fences, there are always cattle getting lost or straying off their home range. So right up until modern times a rancher is liable to butcher a beef not his own. Strict inspection laws controlled by the State Sanitary Board help keep this practice down to a minimum.

Shorty Caraway, who was a stockman for the San Carlos Apaches in Arizona, was a good cook, but he was a cowboy first and any culinary skills he had were passed off as only part of being a hand. Shorty swore all cowboys were good cooks, some were just better than others, was all.

Shorty should know, as he spent years in cowcamps and batched in lonely line shacks before he snared a redhaired nurse to do his cooking for him. Shorty said if he hadn't been able to cook in those days he would have died from starvation.

Shorty started out flunkying for a horse outfit when he was fifteen years old. A "button," the cowboys called him. His job was to do the chores, which consisted of chopping wood, milking the cows, and riding herd on a motley flock of old hens. In between times he was to help out where needed and helping cook was part of his job. Everybody was his boss and when one of the bronc stompers yelled "frog," Shorty was supposed to jump.

There were four or five permanent men on this outfit and they whacked up the cooking chores with Shorty, each man doing his share. There was one man that considered himself the best butcher and took it upon himself to slice and fry the steaks. He took care of the meat which was hard to keep in the summertime. The quarters of beef were hung out each night where they would catch all the cool air available, and in the morning, before flies began their buzzing around, they would be wrapped in a big tarp and put in the shade, or be brought in and stowed under the bed.

Shorty said meals seldom varied much, nor did anyone ever complain. Shorty figured they were "eatin' high on the hog," with steaks and eggs for breakfast along with baking powder biscuits, beans, and "lick" or honey. Once in awhile they would have onions and potatoes. There was always dried fruit, mostly apples and peaches. Shorty said the outfit had gotten burnt out on prunes sometime before he got on with them. That was just fine with Shorty. He'd already eaten his lifetime share of prunes before he'd left his home in Texas.

Most every day Shorty would put on a roast or chop up some ribs or boiling meat. The menus were varied with steak and sometimes chili con carne if the meat was getting low, but before they ran plumb out of beef another would be brought in and dressed out. The cowboys never said they were "gonna butcher." Instead they said they "hung up a beef," or "killed a beef." This meat, hung out to dry and chill in the cool night air, only took one or two days before the cowboys considered it seasoned well enough for consumption.

Shorty said he drew back on eatin' meat when it was still a-quivering and had the body heat in it. Not so his Apache friends. Shorty said he'd seen the meat-lovin' Apaches cut off hunks of meat from the carcass before they were even finished skinning it out. Little fires of oak coals were used to roast strips of butcher steaks, or pieces of the big gut, cut in short lengths, barely having the contents stripped out only moments before. Shorty said the approved method the Apaches used in removing offal from the gut was to cut pieces about three or four feet long, and holding one end, slap the gut against a fence post or trunk of a tree. If this took place during a tulapai party, things were apt to get a bit wild. Anybody adverse to flying cow dung had better take to the brush.

Shorty spent the greatest part of his cowboying years on the San Carlos Reservation and said the Apaches butchered their own beeves on the roundup and a more primitive method would have been hard to find. After running an animal down and roping it around the neck, they dragged it to camp and usually knocked it in the head with an axe. Even with uprights available to hang a beef, with block and tackle, the Apaches preferred their way of rolling the beef around in its own blood, guts, dirt, chips and hair. When finished butchering, Shorty said, the carcass always looked like a train had run over it.

After fifty years, the modern Apache still like their beef butchered this way. The beef is never bled, and great clots of blackish blood are interlaced throughout the carcass. The Apaches insist beef butchered in this manner is far tastier and more nutritious. They could be right. White men drain off the best part, they say, letting it bleed hung high in a tree.

If the weather was hot, the Apache meat would last only a day or so. However, the Apache didn't expect beef to keep. They ate it in great quantities and if it looked like some would spoil, they would salt it and hang to dry as jerky. Their jerky was a great deal different from the white man's jerky. The Anglo was wont to cut his meat in long thin strips, against the grain if possible, salt it well and hang it on lines to dry in the sun.

The Apache couldn't be bothered with all this work and instead cut it in chunks, some pieces weighing as much as two to three pounds. These large pieces were hung on brush (out of reach of the countless hungry dogs) on sides of wikiups or on barb wire fences. Meat dried in this manner often crusted on the outside and the innermost would remain soft. If the Apache had a meat grinder (the government issued many of these), they would grind this jerky in preparing it for soup. This type of jerky could not be pounded into flakes as white cooks liked to do.

A good cook versed in the various ways of using jerky could prepare delicious meals from the dried meat. With the use of a hammer or mallet and a hard surface to pound the jerky on (an anvil or sad-iron made good bases), the strips could be reduced to fine flakes, discarding any stringy stuff or fat that might have become faintly rancid. Put into a hot dutch oven with several spoonfuls of fat, this flaky meat would be browned slightly, flour and milk added to make a gravy. Used on sourdough biscuits or even just plain boiled potatoes it was delicious. Served with boiled rice, it provided a nourishing meal. Pounded jerky cooked in boiled macaroni with tomatoes and a little chili made good eating. Jerky added to a pot of pinto beans always improved the flavor. A broth made by boiling jerky was often served as bouillon to convalescents. Then, of course, there wasn't anything wrong with just eating plain jerky.

The wagon boss, while on roundup, usually selected beef for camp, more often butchering a big calf or yearling heifer (spotted or cutback). Then the marrow guts were saved, along with the heart, liver, tongue, sweetbreads, kidneys, and often the brains. This would be made into son-of-a-bitch stew.

There are several variations in preparing son-of-a-bitch stew, but if it does not include from eight to ten feet of the marrow gut, it is not the real thing. Guts give the stew its distinctive flavor. The small gut is filled with creamy pre-digested fluid and is good fried alone, cut in small pieces.

All agree, a person who is squeamish or can't stand the thought of eating an animal's *organs* had better stand a good distance from the kettle. Yet, one time an Eastern dude was observed finishing off a plate of son-of-a-bitch stew with relish. He remarked to one of the cowboys, "That was the most wonderful stew I ever ate. But, I think the cook was a little careless. Something in it looked like guts. However, I would like the recipe so our cook can make some when I get back to New York."

It's odd, but there wasn't a man that knew the recipe and even the cook seemed to have forgotten how he made that certain stew. They just didn't have the heart to disillusion their guest.

Another great delicacy obtained while on roundup was "Mountain Oysters" or "Prairie Oysters." Jack Thorp in his book *Pardner of the Wind* refused to include this range dish in a chapter on "Chuck" with the excuse "it ain't polite to talk about such things." Well, I approve of being polite but feel anything so common as "Calf fries" and eaten in such quantities and with such gusto, in days of yore as well as today, should by all means be included in this chapter. I even entertained the idea of devoting a chapter exclusively to the mountain oyster.

The old-timers can get a faraway and dreamy look in their eyes when they start reminiscing about tossing mountain oysters into the hot coals of the branding fire. When they popped open, they dragged them out with a stick and ate them crisp and hot without salt, along with blood and hair, some ashes, chips and a little cow dung, flavored with sweat, sheep dip, and "smear," and garnished with dust and flies. Time can improve any memory.

However, you take a day's castrating results of a big gather, wash them in cold water, skin them, split the larger ones, and soak them in salt water for an hour. Then drain well, season, roll in flour or cornmeal and fry in hot fat until crisp as fried chicken. *That* is a different story and one that does not take time to improve its flavor. Serve with Waldorf or tossed green salad and sourdough biscuits and you have a meal fit for a rancher. To hell with kings!

There's a private club down in Tucson, Arizona, called "The Mountain Oyster Club," organized in 1948 by Hubert Merriweather, Steve Moorehead, John Goodman, R. C. Lock, J. Rukin Jelks, and Nick Hall.

Some newspapers were reluctant to use the salty name at first when writing about this unique club, and coyly referred to it as the Cattlemen's Club or the M.O. Club. But they finally came around to reality and started using its real name.

Mountain oysters are served on special occasions in the club's spacious dining room in the Pioneer International Hotel. Also on several occasions, art shows of popular western artists have been sponsored by the club, but its main interest is to provide a central meeting place for ranchers and horsemen and those with like interest.

Cowboys seldom tired of beef, but a change was welcomed occasionally in the form of ham, spareribs, or even a mess of trout or catfish. Bob Birdwell, a rancher in Greenlee County, Arizona, remembers a time when he and Dewitt Cosper decided they was "tared" of straight beef and did something about it. I'll let Bob tell the story in his own words.

"It was back in the fall of 1931 the Double Circles had a wagon and crew camped at Clover Well on the San Carlos Indian Reservation. Ol' Henry Rowden was cookin' for the outfit and he was a good cook. He specialized in chicken fried steaks and could cook the best swiss steak I ever et. He demanded and got the best, fattest and youngest beef available.

"Me and Dewitt Cosper run onto a bunch of them old wild hogs along Blackriver. You know there used to be a lot of them wild pigs in that country. The 'Paches wasn't much on eatin' hog meat and in spite of a world of bears and lions feedin' on 'em, they multiplied.

"Me and Dewitt liked to rope same as the next man and every time we choused a bunch of them pigs we'd have a helluva wild chase. They'd duck and dodge like a Texas jackrabbit! And run! Gawd, them pigs could run faster'n a high-lifed cat! Almost impossible to rope one. They'd duck in under oak brush and hide in the leaves. I'll swear you couldn't see a leaf move. But, one day we caught a big old boar with tusks six inches long. We was lucky and roped him right out in the open. Dewitt heeled him but he was so wrathy and mean, I was afraid we'd get our ponies cut up. I had to shoot that old boar before we could get our ropes off him.

"We decided to skin him and pack the meat to camp. Why we thought we needed a change of diet I don't know. Made old Rowden mad I guess, 'cause he boiled that rank old boar meat for a week. Nothing else. Filled all the damned pots. Guess he proved his point. We never butchered anymore wild pigs and taken them to camp."

Bob remembers this incident as being unpleasant but on another occasion remembers the best meal he ever ate. At least it is a meal he remembers with pleasure after over forty years.

"We was movin' a herd of about 400 head of cows to Pima. That first day's drive was to bring us to Bonita Creek where the Circles had a permanent camp. But one damned thing happened after another and we got caught by dark when we was still five miles from camp. Nothin' to do but stand guard and it was in the fall — and cold! Gawd, it was cold!

"Howard Filleman was bossin' the outfit and he rode on to Bonita and came back packin' a big coffee pot and a side of ribs on the front of his saddle.

"We drank coffee all night while Howard roasted them ribs. Just as it started breakin' day we pulled out with the herd. Howard gave each man a big chunk of meat. That was the best meal I ever ate in my life. Gawd, them ribs was good!"

Cowboys like fried meat. And it had better be done! Easterners might like steaks oozing blood but cowboys scorned meat that was too rare, remarking they'd "seen cows hurt worser'n that and get well." Usually cooks cut up all available steaks off a beef, and only ribs were boiled or roasted.

Not so the Apache cooks. They were great ones for making soup. At least they'd never use the meat saw, and to see a steak cooked by an Apache cook was as rare as seeing any eatable bread made by them.

Bob Jones was a stockman on the Whiteriver Reservation and his cook was a dyed-in-the-wool soup maker. One morning Bob had had enough of half-cooked, boiled meat and sent the crew on the day's work while he stayed in camp and cut steaks. He sawed and sweated and piled up a stack of T-bones two feet high. Finishing his task, he indicated the mound of steaks to the cook. "Now cook 'em," he said as he left camp.

That evening Bob rode in anticipating a juicy steak. He glanced around the cooking pots and spied one big kettle bubbling away. Lifting the lid, Bob saw it full of the boiling steaks he'd cut that morning. "I'll be a sonofabitch," he swore, "T-bone floats!"

They wake you in the mornin' 'fore the break of day
Send you on a circle twenty miles away
The grub is bread and beans, an' coffee black as ink
An' water so full of alkali, it ain't fit to drink.

Not by Bread Alone

At the turn of the century there were several kinds of bread commonly eaten by city dwellers as well as ranch folk. The most common were "boughten" or "town" bread, homemade light bread, saleratus or baking powder biscuits, sourdough bread, corn pone, and tortillas.

"Boughten" bread was made in a commercial bakery and considered an extravagance by most, even though loaves sold from five to ten cents each.

Alf Devore, a long time rancher on Cherry Creek in Gila County, Arizona, told me, "Mama baked the finest bread ever eaten I guess, yet when we country kids got a fresh loaf of boughten bread it was like eatin' cake. We'd stuff ourselves unless stopped."

Another old-timer, Sam Haught, who ranched near Payson and branded the Dollar Marks, told me, "Pappy would buy bakery bread when we went to Mesa, and we'd have this bread for picnic lunches on the long trip back to the Tonto Basin. We kids considered boughten bread a greater treat than candy. It was one of the highlights of a trip to town."

Later on, the pendulum had swung the other way and the same old-timers were calling boughten bread "gun-waddin'" and yearning for the good old days when Ma made homemade bread.

Ordinary home "light" bread made by an amateur from dry yeast may not have always lived up to its name. Dry yeast was cheap and kept indefinitely if stored in a dry place. Yet, there were times when even dry yeast was unavailable and sourdough was used.

Sourdough was called the poor man's bread. The starter could be kept going for years on end if need be. It was also called the "wilderness" yeast. Even in the times of Christ, sourdough was used for leavening bread. It is unknown who the first people were that discovered flour, or meal, with water added, and left it in the open, under ideal conditions, to ferment and start bubbling and "working." Hundreds of years later yeast was discovered, and now manufactured yeast has all but displaced the lowly sourdough crock behind the stove.

There is no great secret or sorcery connected with the making of good sourdough bread, even though some cooks would lead you to believe there is. However, it did take skill and unbelievable ingenuity on the part of the old-time cowcamp cook to protect and keep his sourdough starter. The loss of a starter was classified as a major calamity. It might mean a long trip to a neighboring ranch to borrow another, for virtually every meal drew on the starter for loaves of bread, biscuits, and pancakes. Some cooks even made cakes and cookies from sourdough. For additional leavening, baking soda was used. Then baking powder came into popular use, but many of the old-timers held baking powder in the same category as saltpeter. Any man hearing this rumor would, understandably, be reluctant to use it.

The cowcamp cook usually kept his sourdough in a keg or five-gallon crock. Into this container, each day, the cook mixed necessary proportions of flour and water and set it in a warm place to ferment, often taking the well-wrapped keg to bed with him on cold nights.

A story told to me by Jeff Lauderdale, who worked for the JF outfit in the Superstition Mountains of Arizona, points out most vividly to what great lengths a cook would go in order to perpetuate his precious starter.

At that time, and I think it was in the late twenties, all transportation on the rugged JF range was carried on by pack mules. The entire roundup camp was moved via pack train; cook's kitchen, cowboys' bedrolls, horse feed, the whole works.

The trails winding up and over the mountain called Superstition tested the mettle of man and beast. The JF kept a string of pack animals, mostly burros, but there were eight to ten small Spanish mules. These they used the year around not only for transporting the roundup camp, but for packing salt to the far corners of the range as well. Most of the time the owners hired packers, whose only job was to keep the string of mules well shod, and oversee the mounds of pack saddles, kyack boxes, panniers, hobbles, ropes, and other equipment necessary to keep mules on the trail.

At different times old Eli Drackovich, John Bartel, George Martin, Harry McBride, and many others served as keepers of the pack train. Naturally a string of mules of the size necessary to carry on the work of a big cow outfit would have a number of animals classified as "characters," mostly bad. If this were a book on pack mules instead of cooks, a writer would need go no further for source material than the mules owned by the JF over the years.

One, by the name of Rowdy, stands out in the memory of those unfortunate enough to have had dealings with him. Mule-like, Rowdy might carry on in the line of duty for months, acting the part of a perfect pack mule. Then when caution was thoroughly relaxed on the part of the mule skinner, Rowdy would pull his caper.

Herman, an old Dutchman, was cooking for the outfit the year Jeff was in charge of the pack string, and on this certain day the kyack boxes on Rowdy were laden with pots, pans, and provisions. Tucked carefully in a corner of one pack box was Herman's precious keg of sourdough, the cover tied on with a less than clean dish towel.

The dour old cook accompanied Jeff with the pack string, bringing up the rear on a lazy, flea-bitten grey. Several hours out from the JF ranch, headed for the Revis, the trail became extremely narrow and steep. One slip of a shod hoof and an animal could fall hundreds of feet to the rocky canyon below. For several miles Rowdy had been tucking his tail and flinching at imaginary sounds; shying and spooking at shadows or when the breeze stirred a leaf along the trail. When the big blowup came, Jeff saw exactly what caused the ruckus.

Rowdy was directly behind Preacher John, a cantankerous jack who brayed loud and often, when a rock squirrel skittered onto the trail, saw the mules, became confused and foolishly darted between Rowdy's front feet. That did it! The little mule climbed right on top of Preacher John's pack. The Preacher humped up and let fly with both hind feet, catching Rowdy under the chin with one shod hoof.

That hurt! Rowdy spun half around, collided with Little Orphan Annie behind him, and in the melee fell off the trail and tumbled end over end a hundred yards down the mountain. The pack came loose, and pots and pans, knives and forks fell like metallic rain among the chollas and rocks.

When everything quit rolling and the dust settled, Jeff and Herman could see Rowdy was dead — probably from a broken neck, as his head was twisted sharply under his shoulder and not even his tail was twitching.

Jeff felt real bad about losing the spunky little mule, and old Herman was beside himself with grief over losing his sourdough starter.

Tying their horses and Little Orphan Annie to a scrub oak, Jeff started the rest of the pack string on up the trail, while he and Herman attempted to salvage some of the wreck.

Jeff swears they hung by their toenails and gathered up what they could and added it to Annie's pack. Most of the provender was a total loss, and even the pack saddle was split in two. Jeff cut off the rigging, coiled the pack ropes, and told Herman they might as well go on.

Old Herman was still working around Rowdy's body, busy with a pan and a large ladle he'd managed to salvage. Jeff then relates in wonder the scene he witnessed. For old Herman was scraping sourdough that had spilled onto Rowdy's face, covering the little mule's head with a messy shroud. Herman managed to get several spoonfuls of the stuff into his pan and climbed back over the cactus and boulders to his horse, with a triumphant smile on his bearded face.

Next morning, in camp, old Herman served sourdough biscuits to the crew as usual. All except Jeff, who passed.

It hadn't taken this incident to cure Jeff from eating Herman's biscuits, as some months before, when biting into one, Jeff found a hen dropping in the middle of it. Not at all surprising, considering back at the headquarters ranch at Huitt Station, Herman never kept the lid on the flour barrel and with no screens on the doors and scads of chickens, the results could be pretty gruesome, as Jeff found out.

As pointed out before, sourdough must be kept in earthenware crocks or wooden kegs; never in tin or galvanized containers. A good enamel kettle is fine, and one old-time cook was known to keep his starter in a gleaming new chamber pot — a habit that was somewhat disconcerting to the overly imaginative.

Clair Haight, sourdough maker extraordinary, often provided the cowboys with a source of amusement, by forever overfilling his sourdough crock, whereupon it bubbled up and over the sides and dribbled in sticky gobs to the ground. On warm nights Clair was wont to merely cover his crock with a towel and leave it on the open lid of the chuck box. Unsuspecting cowboys might find upon rising next morning their fancy Olsen-Stetzler boots reposing under the chuck box directly in line with the overactive sourdough crock. No one, but no one, would know how them boots happened to be there. After one such experience of trying to remove dried dough from inside a pair of boots, the owner usually slipped them under his pillow at night.

Almost all old-time roundup cooks mixed their dough in a dishpan of flour. Making a well in the middle of the flour, they poured in the starter, additional water, sugar and salt, and began mixing by turning in small handfuls of flour as they spun the pan around. They wouldn't have known how to get a good "scald" on their bread, making it any other way.

I've seen more than one cowcamp cook make his biscuits right in the top of the flour sack. They would then pinch off biscuits and put them in the dutch oven. No mixing pan, no bread-board, no rolling pin. Simple, but try it sometime. It looks easy but sure isn't.

Each cook had his own preference in mixing his bread. Slim Ellison, of Globe, Arizona, told me of a cook that worked for the Bar Elevens, that had an unusual way of mixing his dough. The cook's name was George, and he is long remembered by the cowboys who ate at his wagon. For George suffered from an allergy and sniffed and snorted all through the spring roundup.

When mixing his bread, George liked to put his pan right down on the ground where he would get on his knees and roll up his sleeves and really knead the dough. Meanwhile, his nose dripped like a can with two holes in it. When George stood up he would brush off his knees; grit, cow-chips and dust showered down into the dough. The cowboys called it "George's Drip and Grit Bread."

Sometimes the starter was left too long in the crock and would sour to the point of stinking to high heaven. The cook would pour off some of the old stuff, add a cup of warm water and a cup of flour and be back in business again. Or he might sweeten the starter by adding a pinch of soda. Care had to be taken here, as too much soda would cause the dough to turn yellow and have a bitter taste. Some ignorant cooks put back in the starter leftover pancake dough containing eggs, sugar, and such. In no time the starter became a bilious yellow and smelled like a cross between a skunk and a slaughter house.

Edna Cosper of Duncan, Arizona, told me an account of an Eastern dude who was extremely ignorant when it came to the ways of sourdough. Edna says this dude was vacationing in the ranch country in western New Mexico sometime after the First World War. One day, while out riding, he stopped by an old miner's shack. The only door was closed, and no one seemed to be about. Curious as to the contents of the cabin, the dude peeked in the window. Through accumulation of years of grime, he saw a lifeless form on the small cot in the far corner of the dark room. But, worst of all was the horrible stink of the decomposing body. Even through the closed window the nauseating odor pinched the dude's nostrils with a sickening smell.

Losing no time, the easterner hastened to a neighboring ranch and reported his grizzly news.

"The old man's dead a week at least," the dude said with conviction. "I know that smell. I spent my time in the trenches in the war and anyone that's ever smelled a dead body never forgets it."

Not having seen the old miner for several weeks, the rancher knew it was possible the old-timer had died alone in his isolated cabin. "Sure hate to hear that about old Sidney," the rancher mourned. "He was well liked. Never had an enemy in the world."

Shortly, one of the men was dispatched horseback to fetch the coroner and undertaker from town, a distance of twenty-two miles. Then hitching a team to a light wagon, the rancher and the dude drove to the miner's shack.

The cabin door was not locked and upon entering they found a pile of old soiled clothes on the bed. That took care of old Sidney, but there still remained the horrible stink. They soon found the source of the odor was the sourdough crock behind the stove.

In a few days old Sidney returned from one of his sorties into the hills searching for paydirt, and was quite put out because no one had bothered to save him a starter when they dumped the contents of his sourdough crock.

I've read several accounts of sourdough starters that had been kept going for years on end. But why perpetuate a jug of foul smelling dough when it is so easy to make a new starter from materials at hand, without benefit of boughten yeast? The only reason the chuck wagon cooks hated to lose their starter was because of the time it took to brew a new one. Sometimes it takes from three to five days before a new starter is lively enough to begin using.

At the turn of the century many Swiss and German immigrants settled in the West. Naturally they brought their old ways of doing things, along with their recipes for the best beer this country has ever swigged.

In German farmhouses breadmaking was done only once every three weeks, and such a thing as stale bread was unknown. The bread was put away in a peculiar manner, which preserved its freshness. After removing the fresh loaves from the ovens the Hausfrau would sprinkle flour freely into an empty flour sack, and into this she packed the loaves, taking care to sprinkle flour between them. Tied up, the sack was hung up in a dry place, where it could swing. The day before the loaf or loaves were wanted they were taken out, the flour brushed off, and they were stood in the cellar overnight.

In cowcamps, bread was seldom meant to "keep." Biscuits made in the morning were usually eaten down to the last crumb. Sourdough bread made for noon or supper seldom saw a piece left over to become stale. In the event the cook did find an accumulation of stale biscuits on hand, he could make them into a tasty bread pudding with lots of spices and raisins.

Cowboys when traveling light could cook up a batch of corn dodgers, which besides being highly nutritious, were a good packer. These were also called corn pone or hoe cake and were simple to make. Basically, the idea is to mix boiling water to whole ground cornmeal, with salt and bacon fryin's added. Balls of the stiff batter were baked in a dutch oven until brown. The resulting missiles were hard as rocks and a sure tooth-breaker, but they were high energy food and a person could subsist on them, along with beef jerky and coffee, for days on end.

When the corn dodgers became too hard to chew they could be made into mush and when they finally became too stale to eat, could be fed to the horses. Hardtack, made of flour and water, was another good traveler in pack bags or chap pocket, but was never popular with the cowboys. Tortillas, used almost exclusively by the Mexicans and Pueblo Indians, were not too popular with cowcamp cooks — probably because they didn't know how to make them properly.

Baking powder biscuits were the cowboy's mainstay. All cowboys could make bread, but like anything else, some were better at it than others. Besides being fast, they ensured leftovers that could be used next meal with jerky gravy or plain milk gravy.

So corn pone and baking powder biscuits were made when in a hurry but even these were not fast enough for Uncle Fred Haught, as recalled by his great nephew Alfred Haught of Young, Arizona. Alfred told me the old uncle had an odd way of talking, often repeating parts of a sentence which was a form of stuttering. He was a good worker, energetic, and fast moving. One time in camp he had a good cook hired, but the cook was awfully slow. This particular time the cook was making corn bread and had it in a dutch oven on a bed of coals, and only time would have turned it to a golden brown. Uncle Fred came into camp, in a hurry as always, lifted the lid on the oven and saw it would be some time before the bread was done. He reached over to a kettle of boiling water and poured a dipper full on the baking bread. "Too slow, too slow. We'll have mush we will, we will," and the old man stirred the mass vigorously. Sure made the cook mad, but he was a good sport and partook of cornmeal mush along with Uncle Fred.

Phillip Reno, an ex-sailor, cooked on the fall roundup for the Aztec Land and Cattle Company, and was lord of the pots and pans for one of the wagons working out of Joseph City, Arizona, in about 1914.

The good-natured cook was soon dubbed "Keeno," for no matter what the situation, it was always "Keeno" with the jovial sailor. Being of mild disposition wasn't all that was different about this pot wrestler, for Keeno hailed from California instead of Texas, and if this were not strange enough, he was also a devout Roman Catholic and attended Mass on his infrequent trips to Winslow or Holbrook. No one had ever heard of a Catholic cook, unless he were Mexican, and then if he wasn't he should have been. To top it off, Keeno wore a sailor's cap and white shirts with black sateen sleeve guards, as bookkeepers were wont to wear at that time.

Keeno was young, probably mid-thirties, black curly hair, beady-eyed as a lizard and rotund as a butter churn. And cook! How that little fat man could cook! He demanded, and got, such strange items for the chuck box as olive oil, tomato paste, spaghetti, and on rare occasions he ordered eggs and received them. Bargeman, the wagon boss, obtained yeast in bulk from a bakery in Holbrook, as the young sailor had been a baker's assistant aboard ship and could make golden loaves of bread, delicious cakes, and tasty cookies that rivaled any a mother ever baked. Although the art of dutch oven cooking was new to Keeno, he soon became adept at using the heavy iron ovens, and the Aztec cowboys were on an eating binge like they had never been on before.

As wonderful a baker as Keeno was, it is not his bread or even his cakes that are remembered, but his manner of leaving when he quit the outfit.

There seems to always be a slight catch to anything so good, and in Keeno's case the catch was his penchant for meticulous housekeeping. Keeno kept his camp so clean and was so demanding of the cowboys in maintaining spotless order in the immediate area of the chuck wagon, he soon made several enemies among the rough and tumble crew. They were a tough lot, mostly, and had a reputation to maintain.

Three young cowboys from Bandera, Texas — two brothers and a cousin — particularly took umbrage at Keeno's demands that

ONE MORE BISCUIT —
CCC

STELLA HUGHES — ARIZONA

they remove chaps and spurs when lining up at the ovens for chow. My Gawd! Some of those Texicans hadn't unstrapped their spurs from their bootheels in years. It was argued by some, that if "Whinny Minnie," madam of a Holbrook bawdy house, allowed them to wear spurs when visiting her recreation parlor, why should they have to remove them in a cowcamp, for Christ's sake?

The custom of removing floppy bat-winged chaps (the Texans called them "leggins") had always been observed by the riders when in the chow line, but Keeno's additional rule of removal of spurs was "goin' too fer" in the opinions of most of the crew. Not all, however, as several of the men, enjoying the finest food they'd ever eaten, swore if Keeno insisted they line up at the ovens "neckid as a newborn babe," they'd comply.

On trips to town the young Texans would snub the genial cook and would cross the street in order to avoid him. The amiable Keeno and the horse wrangler (who had no status to maintain) ignored their rude actions and made a game of the situation. When entering a saloon, they let on they did not notice the three Texans abruptly take their leave. There was far from a shortage of saloons, and Keeno and the wrangler could spend a delightful evening just going from one bar to another and watching the exodus of the unfriendly cowboys.

One Sunday morning after attending Mass, Keeno and his partner were strolling down the dusty main street of Holbrook. Suddenly from a second story window of a rooming house came a yell, and several exuberant cowboys, leaning from an open window, poured a pitcher of cold water on the unsuspecting cook.

Keeno didn't even bother to look up, but the highly agitated wrangler exclaimed in wonder. "Ain't you even gonna get mad? Them boys *throwed* that water on you!"

Keeno reflected a moment, "No, they didn't throw the water on me. They threw water on the man they thought I was." Keeno continued his leisurely stroll up the street with the puzzled wrangler at his heels.

The next day, back in camp, Keeno let on as if nothing had happened. About mid-morning one of the Bandera brothers rode into camp to get something from the hoodlum wagon. He ground-tied his horse dangerously close to Keeno's domain. While rummaging in the jockey box, the Texan's horse pivoted around and took the opportunity to relieve himself. He left a large pile of manure, odorous and insulting, not six feet from the cook's fire.

Upon leaving, the young Texan noted the mess and gave a loud guffaw, and spurring away, threw gravel and dirt all over Keeno.

Late that afternoon the crew rode in and found the cook gone. The horse wrangler rode up but stayed on his horse a safe distance away. He informed the men Keeno had quit and walked to town. *Walked!* That was unheard of! Not a man among them would have walked a hundred yards, even if his life was at stake. And here Keeno had struck out on a journey of eighteen or twenty miles, with the country full of good horses to ride. They spent some time discussing the looney actions of the cook.

The wrangler said Keeno had left dinner cooked, and spirits rose as they observed dutch ovens lined up on beds of coals and the huge coffee pot steaming on the fire rack.

The hungry cowboys grabbed plates and cups and the Bandera boys, as usual, were first in line. A large dutch oven, when uncovered, disclosed a mass of fresh horse manure. Subsequent ovens all contained horse manure in various stages of freshness. The coffee pot was half full of urine (probably Keeno's).

The Bandera boys were all for saddling fresh horses and hitting Keeno's trail and hanging him to the first tree. The wrangler had already left, striking a lope, to the mesa where the remuda was grazing.

Bargeman put a stop to plans of revenge and by evening some of the younger men, and all the old-timers, had turned the incident into a rare joke and laughed about it until bedtime. All except the Bandera boys. They left soon after this, going to the Tonto Basin country where two of them settled down and became moderately successful ranchers.

In 1937, Johnny Wiemer, who ranched on Chevelon Creek, then an old man in his late seventies, told me this story of Keeno Phillip Reno. Johnny said the young sailor had come from San Luis Obispo, California and was known by the Wiemer family there.

They wake you in the mornin' 'fore the break of day
Send you on a circle twenty miles away
The grub is bread and beans, an' coffee black as ink
An' water so full of alkali, it ain't fit to drink.

Dee-zerts

One of the finest books written on trail driving days is *The Log of a Cowboy* by Andy Adams. It was first printed in 1903, but later several more printings were made, and can be purchased at most bookstores today. It is well worth reading, and is considered a classic of frontier literature. In doing research for old-time chuck wagon recipes, I naturally turned to writers such as Andy Adams for information. However, all too often our early-day chroniclers left much to the imagination when it came to describing food and how it was prepared. Even Mr. Adams offhandedly says, "We bought supplies for a two month drive," but fails to mention even one item. Another early-day writer — male of course — mentions, "We loaded two pack mules with provisions." Then again we get a faint glimmer of the contents of a chuck box upon reading, "Flour and salt, and such things, were stowed in the wagon."

Will James, in one of his books, tells of a meal he and another cowboy prepared one night while holed up in a cave. It was storming and the wood was wet. After at long last getting a fire started, he said, "We ate a meal such as many kings would often like to've had." Well! They must have been magicians, as further back in the book he mentions having only bacon and rice in their saddlebags. Also, their sole cooking utensils consisted of tin plates and a coffee pot. Oh, I'd give a pretty to have a recipe of that meal!

Another writer tells of knocking over a sage hen with a rock, and the ensuing meal was "sumptuous." Okay, I'll buy that — even though this writer goes on to tell they roasted the hen on sticks over coals, and they had salt to flavor it with.

[44]

One magazine article, printed in 1875, tells of a cow hunt on the Llano plains of Texas, and the author comments, "We ate light on that trip." And then, when they had almost run out of supplies, "We tightened up our belts." At the end of the story he refers to their "high livin'," when they returned to the ranch. So it was left up to a person's imagination, what they ate "light" of, and what they "ran out" of, and what they ate when it was "high livin'."

Thank goodness, not all writers were so vague. Even Andy Adams does not let us completely down, as he devotes almost two chapters to food. He relates in detail the time he found a nest of sixteen turkey eggs. Fresh ones! He put them all, carefully, in his hat, and toted them to the wagon of McCann, the cook, on the trail drive to Dodge City.

There were fifteen men on this drive, and the next morning McCann fried each an egg for breakfast — and, as Andy says, "Dished them out as if he were in the habit of serving eggs every morning."

But, wait. Remember, there were sixteen eggs — so that leaves a lone egg left over — that is up for grabs. Mr. Adams devotes half a chapter, telling of the all-night game of freeze-out poker, to see which lucky man got the egg for breakfast.

Cowboys, in the early days, had an insatiable craving for sweets. It was probably due to the fact they so seldom got to town to stow up on candy or bakery goods. Also, many ranch cooks lacked skills in making desserts, such as pies and cakes — or did not have the proper ingredients. In any event, a good cook that made plenty of puddings, cobblers, cakes, pies, doughnuts or cookies, was apt to be considered indispensable on any outfit. A cook being talented in this line, even if he be the most evil-tempered man alive, was considered better than an easy going cook that seldom, if ever, turned out a tallow pudding or made doughnuts or cookies. An amiable cook — one so lax he would allow the cowboys to line up at the ovens with their leggin's floppin' in the dust — or one who kept a hot pot of coffee ready twenty-four hours a day — or condoned raiding his chuck box between meals — might be considered a marvel. But, unless he was forever making some sweet concoction, labeled "dee-zert," he could never become the cowboys' favorite.

Holloway Jones, a former Texan, once cooked for the Double Circles on Eagle Creek in Greenlee County, Arizona. This was during the time when the outfit ran thousands of cattle on the San Carlos Apache Indian Reservation. He was ornery, and mean, but could make pies that were the best ever eaten. He was a real pie artist, and could make delectable concoctions from the most unlikely materials. He made sweet potato pie and pies from Irish potatoes that rivaled any ever made from the finest pumpkin. His dried apple pie with raisins and molasses was forever remembered by those who ate it. In season, he made currant, blackberry, wild plum, and gooseberry pies. His custard pies — when he had the eggs — were thick, creamy and a delight to the palate. Nor could any woman ever make a vinegar pie as Old Holly made it.

Rhubarb, or "pie plant" as it was called in the early days, was made into pies that were a gourmet's dream. Even just plain old raisin pies, the way Holly built them, were something to write home about.

When cooking at the home ranch, with eggs available and thick cream from the milk house, Old Holly really came into his own. Meringue, referred to as "calf slobbers," browned to a golden hue, would be piled three inches high on creamy butterscotch pies. Or whipped cream, lavishly slathered on tart green apple or other fruit pies.

It was too good to last. Old Holly's disposition finally got him into trouble, and a cowboy shot him in the heel. Not a Double Circle 'puncher, as none that had ever eaten Holly's pies would have even said a harsh word to him. Instead, it was a nonfeeling lout, from a neighboring ranch. Probably picked the fight with Old Holly through jealousy or spite. Anyhow, after a few days in the hospital at Morenci, Old Holly went back to Texas. Though no one ever saw or heard of him again, he was never forgotten. His skill as a pie artist was the criterion used by the cowboys to judge the efforts of other cooks that followed in Old Holly's footsteps, but never quite filled his shoes. Years later, you might hear an old-timer comment, on sampling a piece of pie, "Pert' nigh as good as Old Holly Jones used to make."

Cooking in camp with dutch ovens, outfits seldom had cooks that would take the time and effort to make pies for a dozen or more men. Cobblers were easier to make, and considered by most to be just as good. Dried fruit was the most common ingredient. Sometimes a cook would make a delectable cobbler by combining apples, apricots and peaches, and flavoring with several kinds of spices.

It took a talented cook, indeed, to make a really light cake in a dutch oven. Controlling a constant even temperature with hot coals in the open took a near genius. But, if cooks shied away from trying their luck making cakes, they made up for it in turning out puddings. Rice pudding with raisins added was called "spotted pup," and without raisins it was simply referred to as "pup." Tallow pudding, or suet pudding, was called "a bastard in a bag," or "boy in a bag," and was made with raisins, suet, flour and spices, and put in a sugar sack and steamed for several hours. This was usually served hot with plain white sauce.

An eggless cake, baked in a dutch oven, sliced in half when done, and both pieces smeared generously with jam or jelly, then put together again, and served warm, was an old standby for camp dessert. Bread pudding — made from leftover sourdough bread, with raisins and spices added, was always a welcome sight to hungry cowboys.

A cook that hailed from one of the deep southern states once worked for the Hashknife outfit out of Holbrook, Arizona. He was old and so bent with arthritis, he looked like he was continually searching the ground for a lost article. He is remembered only as "Humpy," but the desserts he made were long remembered. The cowboys were always clamoring for his dried fruit rolls. These he made by mixing up a batch of biscuit dough and rolling thin, spreading any cooked dried fruit he might have on hand. He folded the rolls, crimped the ends, put them in a greased container to steam until done, or fried them in deep fat.

This southern cook also made fried bread in sticks, six to eight inches long and two inches thick. He used his regular bread dough, and dropped the sticks into hot fat in a deep dutch oven. When browned on both sides, they were removed and drained. When partially cooled, the fried bread was rolled in cinnamon and sugar, or slit half open and the cavity filled with preserves or jam.

Old Humpy's cinnamon rolls were gems of the baker's art. Just before the rolls were finished cooking, he made a mixture of sugar and molasses — or brown sugar and lard — and drizzled this over the rolls until lightly glazed.

When fresh apples were available, he made an apple pudding with layers of crumbled bread, brown sugar and thinly sliced apples. Baked slowly in a dutch oven, it had an aroma like a heady tonic. Old Humpy called this Muncy pudding, and none was left to be thrown out.

When I first started this book on cowcamp cookery, I had a letter from an old-time friend and cowboy cook, Slim Ellison, of Globe, Arizona. In answer to my query on how he prepared certain old-time dutch oven favorites, he wrote, "Well, Stella, when I cooked for cowboys, they was pack mule spreads; and anything besides beef, beans, spuds, and dried fruit, was as scarce as grass on Broad Street. Sech az flavors, spices . . . only had cinnamon, vanilla extract and sugar, razins, dry apples and prunes. I made a tallow puddin'. We called it 'a boy in a bag', and the damn fools et it and called it good. Then I made a white sauce with cornstarch and vanilla flavor — sometimes only lemon extract available.

"I guess the reason they ate this stuff was we had no variety of sweets. I used to make a bread puddin' they liked out of cold sour-dough biskits, two to four days old, brake it up, stir it up soft, put in cooked razins or prunes or dried cooked apples, sweeten heavy, can mix with some condensed milk. Don't cook too dry, just gooey. Top it off with sauce, flavored with vanilla or cinnamon.

"Used to be in pack outfits — we had no eggs — sometimes I'd stir up cake dough without eggs, and then pour it over cooked razins and dry apples in bottom of dutch oven — slow fire under oven, and hot lid — sweet dough browned, and they liked it — called it fruit cake. But hungry, hard workin' cowboys liked most anything."

Andy Adams in his book, *Log of a Cowboy*, tells about a winter camp on the Cherokee Strip, where several cowboys were spending the Christmas holidays, alone and far from home and loved ones. Gloom hovered over the camp like a shroud.

Three days before Christmas one of the old-timers drifted in from the Cheyenne country. He had worked on the range before and they all knew him. In the course of the first evening's conversation around the cook stove, this old-timer mentioned he had become an artist on making doughnuts, commonly called "bear sign" by the cowboys. Said he'd acquired the art from a woman down in the Panhandle Country. He modestly admitted he could turn them out, browned to a turn, just sweet enough, and as toothsome as any mother could make.

Right there, the boss of the outfit told one of the men to go out to the stable, and bring in the old-timer's saddle and put it under his bed, and to throw his horse in the big pasture next morning. For as the boss said, "He stays right here until the first green grass in the spring."

The next morning, after breakfast, the boss rolled a barrel of flour into the kitchen from the store house, got out twenty gallons of lard, one hundred pounds of sugar, and told the bear-sign man to go at it.

"About how many do you think you'll want?" asked the old-timer.

"That big tub full, won't be any too many," answered the boss. "Some of these fellows haven't had anything like this since they were little boys. If this gets out, I look for men from other camps."

By ten o'clock the doughnut maker began to turn out beautiful gems of the baker's art, like he said he could. By dinner the initial taste had made the cowboys ravenous for more. After dinner, the bear-sign man settled down to doughnut making in earnest.

During the afternoon, a boy rode by on his way to the railroad with an important letter. He said he could only stop for a moment, but after eating doughnuts for a solid hour, he filled his pockets and rode away. One cowboy called after him, "Don't you tell nobody what we got."

Late that evening, the boss told the doughnut maker to knock off, as he had been at the stove since morning.

The next day, the old-timer began making bear signs once more. About ten o'clock, two men rode up from the north, which the boy with the letter had passed the day before. Both men made a beeline to the bear-sign tub, which was dead giveaway — they were on to the racket. An hour later, another man showed up on a lathered horse, having rode twenty-five miles since early morning. Making his way to the tub, he refused to sit down like a civilized man, but stood up close and picked out the ones which were a pale brown.

Rolling up his sleeves, the bear-sign man mixed another batch. He had reduced his work to a science by this time. He rolled the dough, cut it, and fried the fine brown doughnuts to the satisfaction of all.

Early in the afternoon, three more men rode in. The doughnut maker's fame was circulating faster than a secret among women. The old-timer never let up, yet by nighttime he had never covered the bottom of the tub. When he finally quit for the night, the remaining ones were soon gobbled up.

The next day was Christmas, and the doughnut maker stirred up a large batch of dough before breakfast. It was a good thing he did, because early that morning a rancher and four of his men rode in from the west. They said they'd simply come over to spend Christmas, but there was no doubt that the word had gotten to them, as they wasted no time gathering around that tub.

As they were all sitting down to dinner, in came two men from thirty miles south on the Cimarron. Like the rest, they used the excuse of dropping by because it was Christmas. The boss called the doughnut maker behind the house, and told him he could quit if he wanted to — but he wouldn't do it, and right after dinner turned out another batch.

The new arrivals hadn't near satisfied their craving by bedtime that night, but sometime the next day, the doughnut maker finally filled his tub. Too bad no one bothered to keep tally. Worse yet, no one took the time to write down the recipe.

It took an ingenious chuck wagon cook, where milk and eggs were nonexistent, to dream up a variety of desserts for the youthful cowhands.

Nobody knows who first made a vinegar pie, but any old-timer can still get misty-eyed when vinegar pie is mentioned. There were two kinds. One required eggs, and was a custard pie. The other was a cobbler, and was best cooked in a dutch oven and was eggless.

A really good recipe of an eggless cake was always prized by roundup cooks, and a recipe calling for neither eggs, milk nor butter was handed down in a family, and considered priceless.

When an outfit ran short of sugar, a good cook could turn out pies and puddings made from molasses, honey, or syrup. Clair made dried apple pies, using honey and spices, and those that were fortunate enough to eat at his wagon swore they were better than those made with sugar.

Clair also made a cake from chopped pork, when available. This cake called for neither eggs, milk, or butter, but used instead molasses, brown sugar and water. It did call for brandy and citron, but these could be substituted for by using whiskey and chopped dried apples.

That was one thing cow country cooks were experts at — substituting.

Oh, it's bacon and beans most every day
I'd rather be eatin' prairie hay
Coma ti-yi-yippie ya yippie ya
Coma ti-yi-yippie yippie ya.

The Lowly Free-holy

As much as I'd like to claim the West was won by meat-eaters, I've got to be honest and give credit where credit is due. More railroads were built, more cattle drives made, more roundups held, more expeditions carried out successfully, and more honest-to-gawd hard work done by beaneaters than any other kind.

The Mexican word for beans is frijoles, and even when an eastern tenderfoot calls them "fry-joles," a Westerner knows what he means. But any way you say it, just plain beans means only one kind to a Southwesterner, and that is the spotted brown and white pinto bean.

No one has, as yet, found a way to degerminate the lowly bean, as they have managed to ruin wheat flour and white rice. So if a person is still interested in a food that is cheap, keeps indefinitely while in the dry stage, is low in fat, high in protein and a fine source of the best carbohydrates, and when cooked improves in flavor each time it is reheated, he'll do well to stock up on sacks of pinto beans. Or white, red, pink, brown or black beans. Whole recipe books have been devoted to bean cookery. Ancel Keys wrote a cookbook called *The Benevolent Bean,* and his work has delicious recipes for every kind of bean under the sun.

Every Westerner has his or her own idea how pinto beans should be cooked and arguments short of shooting wars have been waged on the proper method to prepare beans.

Acey McMillan and his wife, from down Douglas way, made a trip to visit his wife's folks in the deep South. They were wined and dined and after a week of chitlins (Acey was used to eating beef guts so chitlins went down easy), corn pone, fried chicken, and watermelon, which was all fine and good, the day came when Acey got the yen for a meal of just plain beans. So he asked his mother-in-law if she would cook up a batch of beans for a pore 'ol cowboy. That good woman said she'd be glad to comply, and forthwith spent the best part of the day cooking and baking a pot of beans.

Later, returning to Arizona, Acey entertained his cowboy and Mexican friends in describing the meal.

"Gawdalmighty damn boys, here I was droolin' like a hound-dawg, expectin' some good old free-holies and that woman sets out a bowl of them little bitty white beans, all sweetened up with molasses and tomatoes. I was never so let down in all my life. Why, them little white bastards didn't have a good-sized mouse fart in the whole lot of 'em."

Over in California some backyard chefs cook up a pot of big red beans and doctor them up and call them "chili beans." They put in a handful of a concoction called chili powder, which in truth contains more sawdust, cornmeal, and dry horse manure then good red chili. Down in Arizona they know how to cook real chili beans. They ought to, as the best and finest chilies are grown in southern Arizona, more than any other place in the world. This includes New Mexico and Texas.

The lowly bean is largely ignored by our affluent society today, yet dried beans are a food with gourmet possibilities. But, not always.

Any roundup cook that could not boil beans to the proper satisfaction of the cowboys was not considered a good cook. No matter if his bread was feather-light and his steaks toothless tender — if his beans did not pass muster, the cook was apt to be classed low on the culinary scale.

In the Southwest beans were (and still are) considered a necessity. They take the place of the Irishman's potatoes, the Oriental's rice, the Italian's pasta.

The cowboys ate beef backed up with frijoles day in and day out. It was a far greater catastrophe to run out of beans than any other item in the chuck box. Excepting coffee, of course.

Jeff Lauderdale tells of a cook they had on the Hashknife outfit back in the 1920s who has been long remembered for his failure to cook beans properly. This cook was a failure in all other cooking endeavors as Jeff tells it but his ruinin' the frijoles was the most unforgivable.

"We was holding a day herd of 2500 head of dry stuff at Big Tank between dippings (south of Winslow, Arizona). Old Clair

Haight was cooking for the main bunch down on the mouth of Chevelon Creek, so Charlie Wyrick sent up a big 'ol ignorant kid that said he could cook. This kid was so lazy he would use the dishwater over and over again an' when it was cold it would congeal like a pan of jelly.

"Cattle was so poor it was hard to find a beef to butcher unless we made jerky. We might have stood this kid's cookin' if he'd been able to boil beans. He never put any bacon rinds or salt pork in his beans. Nothin'. Not even salt. Nor did he ever cook 'em done.

"After we'd been puttin' up with the slop he dished out for about ten days, along comes a hobo band of sheep driftin' in. They watered out at Big Tank and was supposed to move on to the Mountain (Mogollon Rim), but me and Lovey and Gallopin' Sam (all reps) made a deal with the two Mexican herders. We told them they could stay on the nearby grass if they would let us eat with them.

"Man! Them herders could cook beans. Each night they'd bury an eight pound lard can in a bed of hot coals and next mornin' dig 'em up for breakfast. Along with mutton chops and tortillas we was really eatin' high on the hog. Then Charlie Wyrick came back and started to run the sheep off.

"Lovey told Charlie if he ran the sheep off he and Sam would cut out and go home. They were depending a lot on reps that year so Charlie said he would have to make the sheep move on, but promised to send a cook out.

"The next day Charlie drove up in one of those old time Buicks with the high wire wheels and unloaded Clair. It's a wonder we all didn't die the next few days from overeatin'."

Although most southwestern cowboys like their chili and beans on the warm side, occasionally a cook would get heavy handed with the chili and as Jeff said, "We'd all have a bad case of Mexican heartburn."

Jeff worked for awhile over in New Mexico for the V Cross T outfit when they were gathering to move to Arizona. They had a Mexican cook called Quemado Charley.

"Ol' Quemado used more hot chili in his beans than anyone I ever heard of in my life. He used this firey stuff in everything he cooked — even rolled his steaks in chili. I like chili a lot, but that was even too much for me.

"One evenin' Dee Marley was standing by the chuck box watching Quemado mixing bread dough. Dee reached over, dipped into the chili box, got a handful and dumped it into the dough. I'm sure there would have been a hell of a fight if Dee hadn't looked so mean. Ol' Quemado resented the chili in his dough, but Dee just said, 'You've got chili in everything but the bread and coffee, so why not have it in everything?' "

Any old timer that has been "over the hill where the owl hoots" has a story concerning beans, sometimes humorous, sometimes sad.

I think the saddest bean story I ever heard was told to me by Lafe Cox. It happened back in the early days down in southern Arizona where the wood supply is practically non-existent. I'll let Lafe tell you what happened.

"I was cookin' for an outfit that was always out of beef. Consequently I had to cook more beans than anything else. Took all day to scrounge up enough wood to cook beans with. On roundup everybody contributed by draggin' in chunks of scrub palo verde, roots of greasewood and even dried cholla roots. Sometimes we'd find a fair supply of mesquite chunks and I'd make it last as long as I could for bakin' my biscuits.

"That fall it started in a-rainin'. It rained cats n' dogs for ten days. I mean the outfit was waterlogged to the core. It got harder and harder for me to manage to cook with what sorry wet wood we could find. The boss finally got the brilliant idee of sending the wagon to the railroad to see if we couldn't pick up some ol' discarded railroad ties.

"One of the boys was gone the best part of one whole day and came back discouraged as hell. He'd managed to locate three old ties, full of cresote and tar. Better'n nothing, so I put on a big pot of frijoles. Protected my fire the best I could and used up them ties a-cookin' my beans. Black smoke from the tar turned me brown but the smell of them good 'ol frijoles made up for it.

"The crew rode in late that evenin' wet and grouchy but when they sighted them beans a-bubblin' away their spirits rose somewhat.

"It was still a-rainin' and the camp was slick and sloppy as a hawg waller. Time to remove the bean pot from the fire, I grabs a-holt of both handles and heads for the cook tent. My feet slipped and the pot flipped out of my hands and turned upside down in the mud. I mean I was a-grabbin' for it all the way to the ground. It was a total disaster. Not one of them beans coulda been scraped up out of that mire.

"I sat down and never come so near cryin' like a baby in all my life. The boys seen how bad shook up I was and acted real nice about the catastrophe. They ate cold canned tomaters and biscuits and joked and laughed like fools about the way I'd looked followin' them beans to the ground. Pretty soon I saw the humor of it and we whooped and hollered and kidded about it all evenin'."

There were other things that could happen to beans besides dumping them in the mud. Howard Filleman told me about the time he and Frank Balke were camped up on the mountain near Blue, Arizona.

"We had our camp set up with a tent in the pines. Plenty of wood and good fresh water from the river. We was trappin' wild cattle and gone all day every day. We'd do our cookin' at night and about three times a week boil up a pot of beans. They kept fine for a day or so in the high cool mountain air. During the day we'd sling the bean pot from the limb of a pine tree and each evenin' when we rode in we'd put the beans on the fire and boil hell out of 'em for awhile.

"One night we rode in late and het up the beans and ate by fire-light. Them beans tasted particular good that night. Never had the chunks of salt pork been so tender and flavorsome. Next mornin' Frank got to stirrin' around in the beans and discovered the back-bone of a big 'ol lizard we'd cooked in 'em the night before. Cain't say as it hurt us none. However, I doubt if lizard meat will ever become over popular as a seasonin' for beans."

This coming into camp and heating up the beans without checking on the loose lid caused another unpleasant situation. Howard tells how it happened.

"Well, you'd think after the lizard incident we'd learn — but we didn't. 'Cause a few weeks later we sat down to supper of beans and this time I only took one bite and spit them out. Talk about a rank taste! We inspected them beans under the lantern light and that pot was full of the biggest bunch of greenhead flies you ever saw. After that we was more careful how we put the lid on the bean pot when we left camp in the mornin's."

During warm weather beans are apt to sour in a few hours if not kept in a cool place. Boiling leftover beans once a day for thirty minutes or so makes them safe to eat. Eating spoiled beans can produce some dire results. The O G Rail outfit owned by Babbitt Brothers of Flagstaff once had the entire roundup crew laid low when the cook served up a pot of sour beans. All the men came down with dysentery and suffered such misery most of them were unable to leave camp. Bed rolls were scattered under available shade and near convenient bushes.

Years after this unpleasant episode, Milo Van Winkle told me about it.

"The damned cook was the only one that didn't get sick. He was a cranky so-in-so and some of us suspected he knew them beans was sour. We all had the habit of dousing our beans with hot chili sauce thinned down with vinegar and none of us would have recognized a spoilt bean if we'd met one in the middle of the road."

Milo's brother, Jimmy Van Winkle, along with Wiley Lacy, Joe Jackson, Earl Carter, Slim Ellison and Earl Swan were immobile for three days until Milo rode to the Indian village of Cibecue for medicine.

"In a day or so I got to feelin' better but I think some of 'em mighta died if I hadn't been able to buy about fifteen bottles of a patent medicine called Baby Percy, put out for babies with the 'summer complaint.' Them boys thought I was crazy packin' all that baby medicine to camp. But seein' as how they was weak as infants they drank all fifteen bottles and within twelve hours was back in the saddle again. I might add this Baby Percy medicine is still on the store shelves on the reservation. The Apache women have always taken great stock in it for their sick papooses."

When I asked Slim Ellison about this incident he remembered vividly after almost half a century.

"Stel, I know this is a delycate subject, but you know cowcamps never had no sich thing as toilet paper. Why, even at home, with all the comforts, we used mail-order catalogs or corncobs in the back house. So you kin imagine how hard up we was in camp! Pert' nigh run out of gunny sacks before that baby medicine plugged us up enough to go back to work."

Emmett Hughes and Ed Wiggins once cured an old Navajo chuckline rider from pestering them. Ed loved to tell the story and never had any qualms of guilt for his part in the deed.

"We was ridin' for Ol' Bob Benton and stayin' at John's Draw thirty-five miles north of Winslow. We had to do our own cookin' and Ol' Bob was notorious for supplyin' his men with skimpy fare. So we ate straight beans and salt pork all spring and summer.

"One old Navajo named 'California John' sure liked our grub because he just happened to 'drop by' about five times a week on some pretense or other — mostly claimin' he was lookin' for stray hosses. He was a real nuisance, as every moment he was in or near camp he had to be watched with a hawk eye, for he'd pack off everything not nailed down.

"One day we had a big pot of beans spoil on us and here comes Ol' John just when Emmett was about to dump 'em out. We served 'em to the old camp beggar instead.

"After that we didn't see him for a week. Was beginnin' to think maybe we'd killed the old boy — but no, here he comes lopin' up one day. He wasn't too pert — in fact he was still a little shaky and pale around the gills. Me and Emmett both was real hospitable and asked him to eat with us. We was havin' beans as usual. Old John declined. Said 'Me not hungry. Just coffee.' and he never did eat with us again. He finally quit comin' all together."

One time in the late thirties I was camping with the Benton outfit over on Cottonwood Wash out of Winslow. Mack was foreman of the spread then and sent Ed Wiggins to camp early to help me in any way he could. After chopping up a pile of cedar wood I gave Ed the sack of beans with instructions to "pick" them so I could soak them for cooking the next day. Ed was an avid reader and grabbed a Western story magazine off his bed and lay down beside the pan of beans and absently began going over them while he read his story. When I told him he was the most casual "bean picker" I'd ever seen he told me, "Well, what's fair for one is fair for another" and continued reading his shoot-'em-up story.

Jack Thorp, a collector of cowboy songs and range ballads once was inspired to write an Ode to the Bean.

> I've cooked you in the strongest gypsum water;
> I've boiled you in water made of snow;
> I've eaten you above the Arctic Circle,
> I've chewed on you in southern Mexico.
> In the campfire, on the stove, or in the oven,
> Or buried in the ashes overnight,
> You've saved my life on more than one occasion . . .
> Oh, frijole bean, you're simply out of sight.

Ole Greasy, in town, tanked up on "red-eye"
An' back at the wagon swore he'd die.
The cowboys got as gant as a sandhill crane
Before Ole Greasy could cook again.
The boss got madder'n a wet hen
Swore he'd fire Greasy if he done it again.

Whiskey and Cookin' Don't Mix

This little ditty is sure a long way from being a Pulitzer Prize winner, but anyone the least familiar with cowboy vernacular knows a sandhill crane is mighty thin and gaunt due to a scarcity of suitable edibles in an arid land. "Red-eye," of course, was and still is, a popular term for strong drink, usually applied to whiskey. "Tanked up" means the cook overindulged. And surely, nothing could be "madder'n a wet hen." So there you are — six short lines, with only a little imagination needed to fill in the details — with an episode written about a roundup. For when the cook (any Westerner knows "Greasy" is a camp-cook) returned to the "wagon," you were informed roundup was in progress, because cowboys ate at the wagon (chuckwagon) only when away from camp or the home ranch.

Drinking on the job was seldom tolerated, yet there were times when roundups had occasion to put up with a drunk cook. Certainly most outfits had a jug of whiskey stashed in the chuck wagon — to be used for snakebite or possibly a hot toddy if someone came down with a chill or the flu. No one ever dreamed of snitching this medicinal brew, and as it usually was a "fur piece" to town where whiskey could be purchased, the cowboys and the cook could wait out a dry spell and would make up for lost time the first trip to town. Anyone that couldn't lay off hard licker for a few weeks or a month was classified as a "boozer," and wouldn't have been hired in the first place.

There are always exceptions to the rule, and any old-timer can relate a tale or so concerning a drunk cook. Howard Filleman, a rancher on Eagle Creek north of Clifton, Arizona, remembers one drunk cook he observed in action, when Howard was just a little boy.

Howard says it was back about 1903, when he lived with his folks in Rice, which is now known as Old San Carlos, and covered by the waters of Coolidge Lake. The railroad followed the Gila River, and at Geronimo shipping pens had been built for the use of numerous cow outfits. In the fall, thousands of cattle were shipped from these stockyards by the Three C's (Chiricahua Cattle Company), or as the cowboys usually called it "The Cherries." It was at the camp of the Cherries that Howard and his brother Joe, and Tee Hinton, went one day. All three boys were in the neighborhood of eight or ten years old. I don't imagine the cook let out three cheers at the sight of his young visitors, but as he had been partaking of much cheer from a bottle, he did set them up to coffee and cold steak.

How the cook happened to be in possession of a jug, Howard did not say, but it was soon apparent he was as stewed as a boiled owl. He was cooking dinner for fifteen men, and the boss had brought out a case of canned oysters and several gallons of milk, with instructions to make an oyster stew. Now, this was rather fancy food for a cow outfit, but at shipping time, with long hours and short tempers, oftentimes owners would go out of their way to provide goodies for the overworked men. If the weather was hot, some were known to buy chunks of ice and set out buckets of ice cold lemonade. Ross Santee tells of one time, while shipping at Cutter, that Newt Robinson sent out several freezers of ice cream from Globe. On that occasion they had an Apache flunky, and Ross noted he had never seen before, or ever expected to see again, as much ice cream eaten in one day by one man, as this Apache managed to stow away.

Well, at Geronimo this day, it was cold instead of hot, and threatening to snow, and oyster stew was what the boss had in mind to warm the bellies, as well as hearts, of the hard working cowboys. With town so temptingly close, a man might bow-up and quit at any time and leave the outfit shorthanded.

This cook had his oyster stew in a big open pot, about the size of an eight quart canning kettle. When the stew was ready to remove from the coals, the cook staggered up, but overshot the kettle; and to keep from falling into the fire, he stepped back and planted a big, brogadoned foot right into the hot stew. He let out a howl of pain, and hastily removed his shoe and tore off the sock. After seeing he was not too badly burned, he wrung the stew from his sock, dumped bits of oysters from his shoe, and put them on again.

He finally pulled the kettle from the coals and was pleased to note little had been spilled in the mishap. About this time, he observed the snickering and giggling boys. Picking up an ol' gonch hook, he threatened to skin them alive if they ever breathed a word of what they had seen.

Did he serve the cowboys the oyster stew? As one old-timer once answered to an obvious question, "Does a cat have a climbin' gear?"

Then there was one outfit down in the southern part of the state that once hired on a cook named "Chili." He wasn't the best cook in the world as he felt it his sworn duty to live up to his nickname, and doused everything but the dried apples with a fiery hot sauce. As most of the crew had been weaned on a chilipod, no one complained as long as there was plenty of beef and beans.

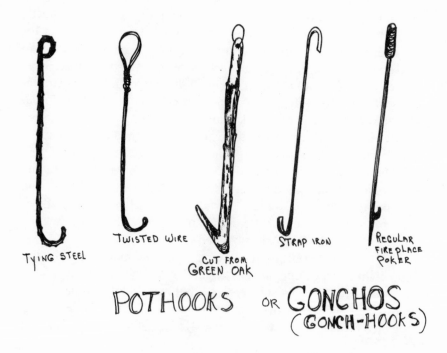

TYING STEEL   TWISTED WIRE   CUT FROM GREEN OAK   STRAP IRON   REGULAR FIREPLACE POKER

POTHOOKS OR GONCHOS (GONCH-HOOKS)

One day, while the entire crew was on a long drive, a gypsy wagon traveling through the country stopped by Old Chili's camp. Nobody really knows what happened, but from pieces patched together later, it seemed the cook traded off a hindquarter of beef for a gallon of blackberry wine.

It was probably several hours after the gypsy wagon pulled out when the boss and two riders topped a low ridge a hundred yards from camp. They were greeted with a volley of shots from a 30-30 rifle held in the hands of Old Chili.

The tune the bullets made as they sang past their heads didn't sound like a love song, and they beat a hasty retreat behind the bow of the hill, where a parley was held. Tate Robins was range boss of this particular outfit, and a calmer man under fire would have been hard to find.

"Now, what could'a happened to that old thang down there?" Tate mused as he dismounted and loosened his cinch.

One of the cowboys, Shorty Feld, came up with an idea of a flag of truce. Maybe Ol' Chili thought they was hoss thieves, or something. So he removed his shirt, broke off a tall sotol plant, fastened his shirt to it, and crawled cautiously to the top of the hill, and hopefully waved his flag. Old Chili planted two nice round bullet holes in the shirt before it could be lowered.

Tate called off further peace negotiations and retired to the bottom of the hill, where they were soon joined by the rest of the crew. One of the men, on vacation from his studies at the University of Kansas, got off his horse and worked his way up the hill, keeping a scrub mesquite in front of him as protection. He was able to observe Old Chili, and after watching for a moment, he made his way back to the group. "That cook looks inebriated to me," he observed.

Shorty had just donned his newly airconditioned shirt, and gave the Kansas dude a scornful look. "EE-nee-bre-ated, hell!" he swore, "that cook's drunker than seven hundred dollars!"

"Well, boys," the boss drawled plaintively, "he's still shootin' too straight. We'll just have to set this one out for awhile, until one of three things happens. He'll either shoot himself, run out of shells, or pass out."

The story has a happy ending. Old Chili passed out before he shot himself or anybody else, but not until he'd used up two boxes of shells and held the hungry cowboys off until sundown.

Cooks could get into a peck of trouble when they went to town. A case in point is a story told about a Hashknife cook back in the eighties.

Abe Lark was thin and dried up as a piece of jerky and just as dark. He was an emigrant from Austria and Lark didn't happen to be his real name. In about 1885 or 1886 the Austrian was a cook for the Aztec Land and Cattle Company, better known as the Hashknife outfit. At shipping time in the fall the outfit camped across the Little Colorado River a mile or so from Holbrook, Arizona. During these hectic days of frenzied activities that cow town got too tough to curry below the knees. With other outfits shipping at the same time, the streets were crawling (literally) with cowboys out to wring the last drop of pleasure to be found in the bordellos and saloons south of the tracks.

When the last steer had been prodded up the loading chute the Hashknife crew lit a shuck for town. All except Abe Lark, who had to set his sourdough, put on a huge pot of coffee, soak the frijoles and tidy up his camp. By the time he had waded the shallow river and walked the mile to town (cooks seldom had a saddle or a horse) his lips were dry and so was his throat.

The old Pioneer bar was enjoying a land office business and this is where Lark ended up. By midnight so many cowboys were riding their horses into the saloon it looked like a livery stable with mirrors. Abe was bellied up to the bar, but because of the celebrating riders, found it hard to carry on with his serious drinking. Finally after being jostled about and stepped on by a half-bronc, ridden by a full drunk, Abe registered a complaint to the bartender.

The bar-keep, himself an ex-cowpuncher, gave Abe little sympathy. Swiping the mahogany, he scornfully queried of the cook, "What the hell you doin' in here *a-foot*?"

His feathers ruffled like an old setting hen, the cook purchased a bottle for the trail and left the saloon.

Back in the Hashknife camp Tom Pickett was sound asleep in his soogans not far from the chuck wagon. Close at hand were his pair of six-shooters and cartridge belts. The Lincoln County War over in New Mexico had only just ended, and Pickett had taken part in the fighting there. In the fracas he had sustained a leg wound which was slow to heal, and because of this was driving the chuck wagon instead of riding. Pickett was a good cowboy but considered tough and quick on the trigger.

About three in the morning he was rudely awakened by sounds of something disturbing the dutch ovens and pots. Thinking it was a horse or stray steer that had wandered into camp, Pickett pulled on his boots and buckled his gun belts around his waist (just in case), and cautiously investigated the cause of the commotion. Pickett had not survived the bloodiest range war in history by being rash or careless. Scouting around the far side of the wagon he finally was able to skylight a form of a man crawling on his hands and knees.

Some dirty low-down skunk was slipping up to kill him while he slept peacefully in his soogans, was the first thought that flashed through Pickett's mind. Drawing his gun he cocked it and the sound brought on a string of curses. Pickett then realized the cook was returning to camp drunk.

Gathering some pitch chips, the cowboy threw them on the still glowing coals and soon there was light to see by. And the sight before him was most astonishing to behold! There on the ground was the little cook as stark naked as a newly-hatched bird and almost as blue. His skinny shanks and thighs were covered with long red scratches, proof the little Austrian had spent some time in the mesquite thickets along the river bottom.

Abe was in bad shape, his wet hair stringing into his eyes and his teeth chattering like castanets. Pickett found a blanket and wrapped it about the shivering cook and led him to a seat near the fire. He relieved him of the bottle still held tightly by the neck and poured himself a drink. Deciding the cook had had enough of "redeye," he gave him a cup of scalding hot coffee instead.

When Abe could finally talk he told Pickett how he had lost his clothes. At least he told him how he thought he had lost his clothes.

"When I got to the river it had come a rise. Anyhow, it looked like it to me." Abe shivered and took another sip of the steaming coffee. "When I went in this evenin' I only had to roll up my britches and carry my shoes. But, with this rise . . . I decided to take off all my clothes. I tied them in a bundle and hung them around my neck. I musta got into some quicksand . . . anyhow I got down. And well, I don't know just where I lost my bundle." The cook finished sheepishly.

"You didn't lose your 'hair off the dog,' " Pickett wryly motioned to the half-empty bottle.

As it turned out Abe Lark had not only lost all his clothes but his wallet as well, with what was left of three months wages plus an I.O.U. from the horse wrangler for a five-dollar poker debt.

Pappy Haught was cooking for the Dollar Marks one fall under the Tonto Rim in Arizona. They were camped at the Wiggens' place and Pappy was doing the cooking in the big cabin. The house was just one long room with a huge wood-burning cook stove in one end and a fireplace in the other. Running down the middle of the room was a twelve foot plank table covered with an oilcloth. The crew ate at this table but all slept in adjoining cabins or in the big barn that was half full of loose oat hay.

Up Willow Creek lived Charley Baker and Perry Stevens, well known bootleggers with a still producing some very potent moonshine. The temptation was too great for some of the cowboys and one evening Mack Hughes, Jeff Lauderdale, Henry Steel, and Hubert Hunt rode up the creek for a visit. They returned before dark with two gallons of high octane "white mule" and a gallon of Dago Red wine.

Back in camp the rest of the crew had just hung up a fat yearling and Pappy was busy cooking a son-of-a-bitch stew. As it happened supper was late due to several reasons, chiefly because it takes S.O.B. stew several hours to cook done enough even for drunks to eat. Another reason for the lateness of the dinner hour was the cook got so drunk he couldn't stay on his feet. In fact Ole Pappy was drunk as a "fiddler's bitch," and so was every member of the crew.

Along late in the night things were getting snorty in the Wiggens' cabin. Pappy had gotten his bristles up over an imagined slight from one of his sons. He soon was "on the fight" and neither Boy nor Sam Haught could calm him down. The more they tried to soothe his ruffled feelings the madder the old man got. Bueford Hunt, Al Parker, and Bill Chilton tried to reason with Pappy, and he must have decided he was outnumbered and as no one would fight with him he turned to leave the cabin. As he came to the end of the table he grasped one end of the oilcloth in his hand and started pulling. He never once glanced back as all hell broke loose behind him. Dishes, forks and knives, son-of-a-bitch stew, glasses, cups, jugs of whiskey and even a pile of groceries stacked on one end of the table all came tumbling off in one awful mess to the floor.

Pappy ignored the bedlam and went right on out the door with the oilcloth trailing behind him like a bride's train and down to the barn where he bedded down in the new oat hay.

Bacon in the pan
Coffee in the pot
Get up an' get it
Eat it while it's hot.

Cooks and Stampedes

The old time Texan called stampede a "stompede," and the word comes from the Spanish *estampida*. But any way you say it, when a herd of cattle, after bedding down at night, jump to their feet quick as scalded cats, and rush headlong in stark terror, the word raises a cowboy's hair on end.

No other subject pertaining to the cowboy has brought on so much in the way of story, songs and pictures. J. Frank Dobie in his wonderful book, *The Longhorns,* devoted thirty-five pages to the fascinating subject of why cattle stampede. It is not my purpose here to relate causes and effects of panic-striken cattle, but to tell several tales of cooks and their reactions to stampedes.

Back in 1923 the Hashknife outfit out of Winslow, Arizona, was preparing to ship a herd of steers. Mack Hughes, then just a kid fourteen years old — a "button," the cowboys called him — was drawing down wages as a cowhand and had been for the past two years. I'll let him tell, in his own words, of the stampede they had one night.

"That fall of 1923 we'd gathered a big bunch of steers to sell. About 1,800 in all. Bill Jim Wyrick was bossin' the outfit and we was camped down by the Clear Creek dam out of Winslow. There was at least twenty cowboys and the horse wrangler. All good cowboys then, and we rode good horses.

"Ernie Burkett was cookin' for the outfit and he had the chuck wagon around a point, near a red bluff. Ernie had cowboyed most of his life, but for some reason or other he was cookin' that fall. Probably 'cause he was a hell of a lot better cook than a cowboy!

"We'd been camped on Clear Creek for a week, cuttin' out cows and calves to sell. There was eight men on day herd, holdin' the bunch between Jacks Canyon and Clear Creek. Each night we penned the two bunches in two great big old corrals hooked together. One was made of page wire and the other was cottonwood poles. Two men at a time rode night guard. Their job was to ride around outside the corrals and keep the cattle awake. We didn't have no trouble other nights as the cows bawlin' and millin' had kept the steers awake and on their feet. But this last night we'd moved the cows and calves to a pasture closer to town and turned all 1,800 of the steers into the two corrals.

"Albert Crockett and Dave Roberts had first guard. Everything was quiet. Too quiet. Some remarked about it bein' a perfect time for a 'run.' About eight o'clock all 1,800 of them steers broke and run. The whole corral was laid flat in a minute and the cattle poured out like a flood. Out aways from the corrals was a little run-down board shack with two old trappers sleepin' in it. The steers hit this shack and crowded it off its foundation. They never slowed down. The shack was knocked over and it slid on its side for fifty feet into a little draw. Damndest job of house movin' you ever saw. The two old-timers wasn't hurt a bit. Just shook up some.

"Back at camp we heard the roar of the runnin' cattle and we started mountin' our night horses! Some of the cowboys hadn't gone to bed yet. Most of us had our saddled horses tied to a fence not far from the chuck wagon. I remember my brother Jim had a buckskin pacer branded Bar W. I don't know why he picked this horse for night duty as the son-of-a-bitch couldn't stand up in the day time, let alone run in the dark. I always picked the best horse I had. This night I was ridin' Biscuit, a white horse branded RH on his left leg. He was sure a good 'un.

"There was a lot of things that happened that night we all laughed about later when we got to comparin' notes. Bill Lovelady was ridin' a horse called old Hendotomi. Somewhere out there among the runnin' cattle old Hendotomi stumped his toe and fell. Scalped both him and Lovey. I mean really scalped! Hendotomi had all the hide from between his ears plumb down to his nose peeled like a banana. It hung down in a strip a foot long. Had to be trimmed off with a knife. An ol' Lovey had scalped his bald head, only not as bad. Other things that happened was Bill McKinsey chased one old spotted steer all night. Came in next morning with just this one ol' steer. Hebe Petti rode herd on a bunch of bushes all night. Thought they was steers. Even sang to 'em. But I guess the damndest thing of all was what the cook done.

"When the cattle first broke to run the cook had already gone to bed under the wagon. He jumps up and runs out and climbs on 'Bulldog', Ben Page's night horse and takes off, whippin' and spurrin' in the opposite direction from the runnin' cattle. Page watched his horse disappear in the night and he threw a fit. Page was a helluva good cowboy, and here that damned loco cook has set him afoot.

"About ten o'clock next mornin' men began driftin' in with bunches of cattle from different directions. Most of the leaders had been turned back about ten miles on Chevelon Creek. When all of us had got in it was discovered the cook was missin'. Meanwhile, Page had cooked up a big bait of grub and was bitchin' his head off because Burkett had stole his horse. Said he'd be damned if he'd go help hunt for him.

"The cook was soon found. He hadn't gone fer. He was at the bottom of the bluff not two hundred yards from camp, crawlin' around on his hands and knees near his dead horse. He'd been knocked silly by the fall and it was a day or so before he plumb got over it."

The most common cause of stampedes is thunder and lightning, but oftentimes the cause cannot be sensed by man. A herd of cattle can be eased onto their bed ground, apparently contented, absolutely quiet. Then in one instant every animal can be on their feet and running in full flight.

Bill Martin, who ran the JF outfit for Clemons Cattle Company for years, said those old steers, gathered out of the boulder pile called Superstition Mountain, liked to run when they hit the desert. Maybe they did, because they seldom failed to do so the first night on the trail to Coolidge, where they were to go in fields to finish fattening for market.

Harry McBride was cooking for this outfit in 1938. That year Clemons was trailing a herd of steers from the ranch at Huitt Station to fields near Florence. Harry drove a team of snorty black mules to the chuck wagon and out on the desert between Florence Junction and Mud Tanks, Harry fell asleep and tumbled off the wagon seat. The mules spooked, threw figure-nines in their tails and ran off with the kitchen.

Bill Martin discovered the absence of the cook and the wagon when the herd reached Mud Tanks that afternoon. Mack Hughes and Dwight Haught were sent back along the route the cook was supposed to be taking, to see what could have detained him. Several miles from the tanks the two cowboys met the mad McBride footing it along the road. His usual florid face was bandana-red and his shirt was plastered to his back with sweat. He was wearing tight, high-heeled boots and the hot desert sun had welded them to his feet.

"My Gawd, I'm glad to see you guys," he croaked as he collapsed under a mesquite. "I cain't walk no futher. My feets' done ruined," and he mopped his brow with the back of his shirt sleeve.

The two cowboys asked in what direction the mules had gone and started off. The cook's pleas were pitiful as he begged them to let him ride double on one of their horses. But as he weighed over two hundred pounds they turned him down. Besides, they pointed out, they were both riding half broncs and finding the mules and wagon was more important then rescuing a cook. After awhile they looked back and saw McBride valiantly trudging on towards camp.

The mules and wagon were found just before sundown hemmed in a fence corner six miles from camp. It was long after dark when the sore-footed cook managed to throw a hot meal together and it was late when all retired for the night.

The steers were penned in a large water lot and just outside the fence was camp. Cowboys, in their bed rolls, were scattered on the far side of the chuck wagon. Everything was quiet and the steers all bedded down. Not a breath of air was stirring. When the moon came up it was so bright the nearby hills seemed to march right into camp. The cattle could be seen, resting on their bed ground, almost as plain as day. Then suddenly with no warning at all, the entire herd was on its feet and running. They mowed the fence down as if it were made of strings, and gathering momentum, they tore right on through camp scattering pots and pans and cowboys in their wake.

The cook, asleep under the wagon, made one herculean leap from his bed and in spite of his excess weight and aching feet, landed neatly atop the tall chuck box.

The moonlight provided such good vision the cowboys were able to gather the herd and put them back into the water lot. They restrung some of the broken wire and returned to camp where they began gathering up their bedding which was strewn for a hundred yards. Nobody went back to bed; instead the fire was built up and horses left saddled. Two men were left on guard just outside the water lot. The cook, whose feet were killing him, went back to bed and soon his snores were echoing in the clear desert air.

About an hour later the cattle ran again. Out through the makeshift fence, through camp and into the desert. The cook lost no time in piling on top the chuck box once again.

Contrary to fiction writers telling of cattle running thirty miles in a night, usually cattle do not run far when they stampede. However, if they are not gathered after a run, they will drift miles during the night. Now the JF steers lost their momentum and stopped and began milling and bawling. Soon the cowboys had them corralled again. This time four men were left to guard the wide gap now existing in the water lot fence. By 2 a.m. all was quiet and the cattle bedded down, seemingly content.

An hour later the herd put on a repeat performance. By this time the cook was so exhausted he could barely climb atop the wagon. When the last steer had passed he wearily crawled back into his bed.

"That does it!" he swore. "I ain't gettin' outa this bed no more. I don't care if the world comes to an end." By the time the herd was quieted once more the cook was deep in slumber, snoring like a choked bull.

Just before dawn there was a rumble and a roar and here comes that entire herd once more. The cook was out of his bed and on the chuck box in one bound, his raw and swollen feet forgotten.

Each time the steers ran, the cowboys standing guard would circle them, bring them back into the water lot and turn them loose. Some of them would barely lie down when here they'd come again. By actual count (the cook's) those JF steers ran six times that night. Such a series of stampedes was unusual.

Ole Slick an' Greasy cooked for the Bar U
He made dough-gods too tough to chew
His frijoles rattled in the pot
His chili sauce was too damned hot
His coffee was bitter as alkali
Mean as hell, he'd spit in your eye
Six-shooter slung low on his hip
No cowboy gave him any lip
We ate his grub sweet as pie
Better do that than to die.

Gun-totin' Cooks

A big cow outfit in the northern part of Arizona once hired a cook the cowboys called Hotair Hill; but not to his face. The waddies eating at his wagon the fall he cooked for the roundup called him Mister Hill. Their politeness may have stemmed from the fact the cook always had his six-shooter at hand. If not strapped on his hip, he had it hanging conveniently on the side of the chuck box.

Although Mister Hill did not actually stir the soup with the barrel of his gun, he let it be known he was plenty tough and a mean hombre. He disclaimed Texas as his home, but no one ever knew where he came from, although he sometimes bragged about the spread he'd left "back East."

Hotair Hill was a fair cook and clean, but he talked constantly in a high thin voice that would have gotten on the nerves of a saint. His mouth was never closed as he even talked in his sleep. Between snores he jabbered and ranted the night through.

Maverick Murdock, the wagon boss, moved his teepee tent a hundred yards from the chuck wagon so he could sleep the few hours allotted a ramrod of a big cow outfit. The cowboys took their cue from the boss and beds were scattered so far into the surrounding brush one of the waddies swore he got lost every morning trying to find his way to the wagon for breakfast.

Hotair seemingly needed very little sleep, as he was last to bed at night and began rattling his ovens at three in the morning. If no one got up, Hotair carried on a lively conversation with himself and his voice carried a mile in the clear mountain air. "Mornin' stars up and ain't even got ol' fire built," he would screech. Then raising his voice a nerve-racking octave higher he'd rouse the horse wrangler, *"Up and at 'em boy! Day's half shot. Rise and shine!"*

Fisher Collins, who seldom said anything, was heard to remark the cook "had the worse case of diarrhea of the mouth" he'd ever seen.

The cook delighted in making a din by slamming lids on kettles, rattling the dipper in the water bucket, beating a spoon on the edge of a pan, or even chopping wood. The whole crew could have stood Hotair's constant yakking, bragging and keeping everyone awake half the night, but the way he could stir up trouble was an art in itself, and when Hotair, by chance, happened to tell the truth it was purely an accident.

Maverick Murdock was a very patient and easy-going boss. He tried to keep peace between the cook and the cowboys but before many weeks had passed two good men bowed up and quit. It was the general consensus the cook was responsible for their leaving.

One morning after a fitful night's sleep, Maverick said in a confidential voice to Fisher Collins, who had only recently joined the outfit, "I'd fire that son-of-a-bitchin' wind-bag if I wasn't afraid of him," he said, half in earnest.

Fisher was tall and loose jointed, sad-eyed and wore a long blonde mustache that drooped like cows' horns. Little was known about him, nor did he volunteer any information. Soft spoken and easy-going, he savvied cows and did more than his share of the work. Maverick asked no more of a man.

When Maverick mentioned firing the cook, Fisher brightened instantly. "Let me do the firin' then," he asked eagerly.

Maverick hesitated only a moment, "Go ahead," he said, "I'll back you all the way."

Now, this was most unusual procedure in the range country. Usually the voice of command started at the top (owner or owners of the ranch), went on down to the manager, who in turn "shot his pills" to the range boss or straw boss. This policy was almost never violated and Maverick was well aware of range protocol, but now he urged Fisher on. "Just watch the bastard," he warned.

Fisher lost no time marching over to the chuck wagon and confronting the cook. "Hotair, you're fired," he said in a loud voice, "An' you can go roll your bed right now."

Hotair gave Fisher an incredulous look and turned to Maverick for confirmation. When Maverick nodded the cook edged towards his six-shooter lying on the chuck box lid. "No two-bit stinkin' cowpuncher is gonna fire me," he said, laying his gonch hook down and suddenly lunging for his gun.

Fisher wasted no time and calmly picked up the gonch hook and rapped the cook behind the ear.

Breakfast was over and the men ready to ride when Hotair "came around." Meanwhile someone had rolled his bed, being careful to place his six-shooter inside it. One of the men saddled Hotair a horse, packed his bed on a mule and took him to the railroad.

Maverick appointed one of the men to cook while he left to hunt up another cook. That night the crew had the first good night's sleep they'd had all fall.

The next cook was a walking wonder. Or rather, a riding wonder, for he arrived at the roundup riding an old sway-backed, flea-bitten grey mare called "Old Mama." A *mare!* No one in the cow country rode mares unless it was some nester kid, and only then because they had nothing better to ride. Not that mares don't make good riding mounts (they do . . . and smart), but a mare turned loose among a bunch of geldings was like putting a lighted punk to a string of fire crackers. They fought over a mare worse than a pack of dogs over a bitch in heat. All night long the thump of shod hoofs hitting empty bellies sounded like tomtoms at a powwow. Next morning there was apt to be cracked ribs and withers with chunks bitten out the size of tea cups.

Maverick had found old Oscar Burlingame at Peach Springs, a little town on the railroad, and had hired him the moment the old nester had said he could cook. No matter if he was a cartoon personified. Stooped and grey, he wore baggy bib overalls that flapped in the breeze like a bed sheet on a clothesline. His old hat sagged fore and aft and was full of holes. He wore brogan shoes whose soles were attached to the uppers with pieces of baling wire. Tied behind the ancient high cantled saddle were a few ragged soogans and the old man's "war bag."

This apparition may have given Maverick some qualms, but after the first meal dished up by the cook, the wagon boss knew they were eating the best prepared food ever cooked on that outfit. What old Oscar did to the T-bone steaks cut from a tough six-year-old steer (butchered because of a broken leg) was a miracle. His sourdough biscuits were so feathery-light a man could eat six and barely feel the weight in his stomach. Although the cook had arrived late in the afternoon there was a large dishpan of delicious doughnuts for dessert. Even the Arbuckle's coffee tasted different.

The results of such a meal played havoc with the cowboys' sleep. Or perhaps it was Old Mama that helped keep the outfit on their toes all night. For Old Mama was a real "camp robber," as her owner had spoiled her rotten by tossing her biscuits, bits of doughnuts, or piecrust. Although hobbled, she roamed the premises all night, tugging at bed tarps and nuzzling lids from dutch ovens, making a clatter in her search for tidbits. The cowboys lost so much sleep some had decided they would have to take to the brush again as they had when Hotair was pot wrestler.

The next day Maverick suggested in his most conciliating manner, that perhaps Old Mama be staked at night. Oscar readily agreed and from that time until roundup ended the outfit gorged on Oscar's pies, cakes, puddings, doughnuts, and cobblers. Not only did the cowboys like Oscar's cooking, they enjoyed the old-timer's wit and good humor. Besides being so easy to get along with, Oscar went to bed early. After staking out Old Mama not far from camp, Oscar would kiss the old mare on the nose and give her a final loving pat, then retire to sleep the night through without a snore.

The first time the cowboys witnessed Oscar's good-night kiss to Old Mama, one of them began to snicker and received a dig in his ribs so hard he sucked in his breath. The rest of the outfit took their cue and after that if Oscar had taken the old mare to bed with him, not a man among them would have lifted an eyebrow.

Gun-toting cooks were the exception and not the rule. Clarence Post of Benson, Arizona, told me a story about another cook that used his gun under unusual circumstances. I'll let Clarence tell it in his own words.

"Bill Smith cooked for the Boquillas Cattle Company (Wagon Rod outfit) down in the southern part of Arizona. There's plenty of cowboys around today that knew Bill Smith and ate at his wagon. All agree he was a damned good cook and easy to get along with. Unless he was recovering from one of his trips to town where he had indulged in too much 'forked lightning.' At times like this ol' Bill could be mighty peevish indeed!

"The sardine story happened at the Stone House on the Wagon Rod range. This camp was about a quarter mile from the railroad and back in the twenties there were a lot of hobos riding the rails. Some people say the bums had a sign they would leave in some prominent spot indicating this was a good place for a handout. I guess the hobos on the Southern Pacific had a good sized billboard, 'cause when the roundup was at the Stone House old Bill fed several free loaders every day. Some of them came by so often the old cook knew them by name.

"I will say this, he paid no favoritism, and handed out good grub to one and all, and was never known to turn a tramp away hungry.

"One day, after a night on the town, Bill returned to the camp remorseful and with a head big enough to eat hay with the horses. He spent most of the afternoon lying on his bed next to the kitchen stove. A hobo Bill knew as 'Frisco showed up and said he hadn't had a good meal in days. Bill got up and rummaged around in the chuck box and comes up with a couple of cans of sardines.

" 'Frisco looked sourly at the skimpy fare and said to Bill, 'This the best you can do?'

"The hobo hadn't ought to have said that. Ol' Bill looks the bum over with his blood-shot eyes and says, 'Yes, I can do better'n that,' and goes to his bed. He turns with that old forty-five and throws down on the bum. 'Now, by Gawd, you eat them sardines and call 'em good.' And Bill waves the gun under that hobo's nose.

"Made him eat six cans of sardines without bread or even a cup of coffee! When the bum had eaten enough of the fish to satisfy the cook he let him go. That was the last time anyone ever saw 'Frisco at the Wagon Rod camp."

They Sure Come Unwound

"Some of them old time roundup cooks was mean bastards," a long time rancher in Gila County once told me. "But, then, some of 'em had reasons to be." Then he related a story about a Bar Elevens cook which I think heads the list of extreme provocation.

Much as I'd like to name names, discretion prevails, so I'll call the cook Ole Greasy and the two cowboys Shorty Long and Bob Jones. Aliases as good as any. If any.

The Bar Elevens outfit at that time was owned by D. V. Marley and the range was leased from the Whiteriver Apaches. Headquarters, if you can call a shack and some rundown corrals headquarters, was at a place called Medicine. The entire range was rugged, rocky, and roadless. Roundups were carried on via pack mules and when moving camp Marley would designate one or two men to help the cook pack. No easy chore and not one relished by the cowboys.

On this particular occasion the cook and his two young helpers had to go into Canyon Creek. The trail was steep and rocky and along the way one of the mules had a mishap and the pack turned under his belly. Kyacks and grub got kicked and strewn around an acre of rocks before Shorty and Bob got the fractious animal caught and tied to an oak tree.

Ole Greasy, trying to salvage some of the scattered provender, picked up a gallon can of syrup and the whole bottom fell out. Gobs of the sticky stuff spilled down the front of the old man's britches. It didn't improve his vile disposition any.

Arriving at the bottom of the canyon they stopped at the usual camp site, a nice little park close by the running stream. While the cowboys unpacked the mules and gathered some wood, Ole Greasy removed his trousers and washed them out in the creek. He hung them to dry on a nearby oak bush and hurried about preparing supper, as the crew would be riding in ravenous as usual.

When the fire was built the cook put on a pot of coffee for himself as well as the cowboys and continued his preparations for the meal. Busy, bending over his pots, his shirttail too skimpy to be very modest, Ole Greasy must have presented a comical sight; for the cook did not have on underwear, and each time he leaned to pick up a utensil, his private parts were exposed to full view of the cowboys.

Shorty and Bob, squatting on their heels close by, drinking their coffee and smoking cigarettes, refrained from making disparaging remarks, as the cook's usual disposition was that of a teased rattle-snake.

Yet, finally the temptation proved too great for Bob. Before he seriously considered the consequences, while Ole Greasy was bent over with his back to the cowboys, Bob drew a slim stick from the fire and the end glowing, gingerly touched the cook where it would hurt the worst.

Ole Greasy's reactions were instantaneous. He exploded into the air, swung around and flattened Shorty to the ground with his gonch hook. He hit him so hard he knocked the surprised cowboy from under his hat. He made another wild swipe at Bob, but that cowboy was crawling on his hands and knees, scrambling to make his getaway. In his wild flight he upset the coffee pot, fell over the fire irons, overturned the sourdough keg, and stampeded the mules.

Ole Greasy gathered a handful of rocks and chunked the cowboys out of camp, meanwhile calling them every vile name under the sun.

Shorty and Bob ran until they were out of breath and out of range of the flying rocks. They finally sat down on a ledge a safe distance from camp and watched the wrathful cook try to restore order to the chaos they had wrought.

Bob let his breath out in a whoosh and nervously reset his hat. "My Gawd, that ol' fool sure come unwound! Who'd a thought he'd get *that* mad!"

Shorty cast his rash young friend an incredulous look. "What in hell did you *think* he'd do? If he'd had a gun he'd have killed both of us!"

Just then D. V. Marley rode up and observing the mess asked the cook what happened.

Ole Greasy indicated the two cowboys with a wave of his gonch hook, "Ask them sonsofbitches," was his terse reply.

Perplexed, Marley rode over to the cowboys. "Who the hell upset the cook?" he asked with a frown. "What happened here?"

"Aw, nothin'," Bob cut his eyes at the boss. "I was just a-tryin' to keep ole Greasy from draggin' his cods through the pots, is all," he explained sheepishly.

Amos Clayton of Winslow, Arizona, was an old-timer himself, in 1937. He told me a story about an old uncle of his by the name of "Chick" Clayton, who was a good camp cook and a well-known character. The old uncle had lost a leg in the Civil War and had a crude wooden leg strapped to his thigh. When he walked, the rigging made a chirping noise reminiscent of the sound of baby chickens. So the cowboys nicknamed him "Chick." I lost my notes to this story when our home burned in 1947, and have forgotten the old uncle's first name, but I haven't forgotten what the cowboys did to old "Chick" when he was cooking for the CO Bars one spring roundup, or the terrible consequences resulting from their prank.

Chick Clayton spent his years after the war on the prairies of Oklahoma Territory and was an old man by the time he immigrated to the rangelands of northern Arizona, which was in about 1908. He soon went to work for the CO Bars, owned by the Babbitt Brothers of Cincinnati, Ohio.

Amos told me the old uncle had, as a boy, suffered a terrifying experience. When rabbit hunting, he fell into a den of rattlesnakes. Though he was not bitten and managed to escape unharmed, the ordeal left traumatic scars and the old man never got over his deathly fear of snakes. I'll let Amos tell you of the incident at the CO Bars.

"Uncle Chick was a big grizzly of a man, with a beard like a fiery bush as he was as redheaded as a cardinal, as are most of my folks. He got a job cookin' for one of the wagons out of Flagstaff. He drove four half-wild buckskin mules to the chuck wagon. You know the CO Bars was a big outfit then and had several wagons workin' different parts of the country. Chick's outfit also had a bedwagon driven by the swamper. This swamper drove four mealey-nosed black mules that could run like greased lighten'. I remember Uncle Chick tellin' about the races they'd have with them wagons and mules. Now, when I say races I sure don't mean they was run over any race track or even down a road. No siree, Bob. They run them races over the roughest damned country you ever saw. An' you couldn't rightly call them heavy wagons racin' vehicles either.

"Take that bedwagon, it would be loaded above the sideboards with eighteen to twenty bedrolls. An' these was *bedrolls,* full of heavy soogans, the cowboy's 'warbag' and his 'thirty years gatherin's.' Not a one of them bedrolls would'a weighed under seventy pounds. It usually took two good men to toss one onto the bedwagon. Then along with all the heavy plunder that went on it, them mules shore wasn't pullin' no chariot.

"Uncle Chick found it hard to get around with that wooden leg but he shore didn't ask no favors of any man, nor did he get any. When he got his teams hitched to the chuck wagon he'd climb to that high seat, release the brake and squall one of them famous rebel yells and them mules would leave the earth. He carried a long raw-hide whip and he'd pop that whip over them mules that sounded like a pistol shot. Them buckskins would lay into the collars and take Ole Chick on the wildest ride you ever saw.

"Now on this spring works was two big, towheaded boys — just big, ole ignorant kids, maybe seventeen, eighteen years old. One evenin', after an early supper, these boys found an ole rusty bull-snake out aways from the cook's fire. They brought it into camp and was tossin' it around and havin' fun. Now, I ain't never seen no cowboy that had much truck with snakes, and certain none in camp, but I mean when Ole Chick sighted that snake he threw a conniption fit. He cussed them boys out in some mighty ripe language, and Ole Chick was noted for his muleskinner lingo. I guess you'd say he not only knowed the words, but the tune as well.

"He told them 'morons,' as he called them, to get that snake out of his sight and never bring another one in camp as long as he was cook for that outfit. The boys snickered, but seein' the deadly gleam in the old man's eyes and the gonch hook in his hand, they did as told.

"Ole Chick went to bed mutterin' about snot-nosed kids hirin' out as cowboys. Next mornin' things seemed normal and after break-fast was cleaned up Chick got his mules hitched and ready to go. One of them two boys helped break camp and was on hand when Chick climbed to the seat and released the brake. He let out a squall an' at the same time reached for his whip on the seat beside him. But, instead of the long whip, coiled there was this ole bullsnake.

"When Ole Chick saw this snake in his hand he screamed like a woman. He dropped the snake and it fell into the wagon box at his feet. Meanwhile, them four buckskin mules thought this was gonna be the greatest race ever run, as they'd never heard the cook yell at them in that tone of voice before. They took off like the clatter wheels of hell an' in nothin' flat was runnin' like turpentined cats, their ears laid back and their eyes a-rollin'.

"Ole Chick wasn't about to share his wagon with no snake, an' as the Mexican says 'he let 'em went to hell.' He just throwed them lines away and bailed out. Maybe it's a good thing he quit 'er when he did too, 'cause not a hundred yards from camp them mules hit a ditch and turned the whole caboodle over. The tongue run into the ground, broke off, the doubletrees come undone and them buckskins was hog-wild loose.

"That there kid took off after them runaways, but he didn't have no show a-tall of catchin' 'em. They just left him like he was standin' still.

"The runaways was slowed down a little when they caught up with the remuda. The hoss wrangler heared 'em comin' and built a big hungry loop and managed to rope one of the leaders. He hadn't ort to a-done it, for tryin' to stop that bunch was like tryin' to stop a freight on a downhill grade. His pony was jerked down, his riggin' broke and that poor little hoss was pert' nigh killed.

"This whole wreck stampeded the remuda and they scattered like quail. One of the cowboys later told me it took a week findin' some of them hosses and two days pickin' up pieces of harness and tryin' to patch the whole works so they could finish up the brandin'.

"Poor ole Chick, when he jumped from the wagon, broke his leg. Hell no, not his wooden leg. His good leg. Real bad too. Not only that but he kinked his neck. Permanent. He carried it cocked to one side for the rest of his life. The Babbitts sent him on the train to a hospital in Los Angeles and he was out there most of a year.

"Them there boys sure caught hell from the wagon boss, but they denied puttin' that snake on Chick's wagon seat. No one ever knew for sure if they really did or not. It's possible the snake coulda crawled up there. But damned improbable."

Charles M. Russell tells in his book *Trails Plowed Under* about a chef of the Sour Dough School who cooked a vinegar pie. This was in a wood-burning stove and while the pie was cooking in the oven a friend put some Giant powder in with the pie to thaw out. When the powder blew up it scattered pie, the cook, and the shack for a mile or more.

Well, Pete Cobb didn't put powder in the oven with a pie but he almost blew Charley Maybre and his stove to kingdom come one time when he was working for the Double Circles on Eagle Creek in Greenlee County, Arizona.

Pete was a big, chuffy red-faced Texan, a good cowboy but a shade wild. When he told me this story in 1944, he may have shaded it a bit in his favor but I'll tell it exactly as he related it to me.

The old Double Circles had good stout ranch buildings, most of them made of adobes with walls over two feet thick. Chief Maybre was cook and the kitchen and dining room were housed in a building over forty feet long. Chief cooked meals for a dozen cowboys on a big black range called "Southern Comfort." He was sure proud of the big stove with its huge firebox and spacious warming oven.

On the occasion of the big blowup a bunch of the cowboys had been to Clifton on a spree and returned early one evening with several jugs of "white mule" and continued their celebrating long into the night. The boys waxed very merry indeed and the booze jug was hoisted and the fiery stuff passed their lips by the gallon. The boss was absent at the time so the party was extended into the next day, with some of the boys still able to ride, going up the creek and replenishing their jugs from a local bootlegger. At the end of the second day the party had all the earmarks of turning to a brawl.

Pete said Slim Nichols and Marshall Lewis got into a less than friendly argument and some thought there might be a shooting scrape. Charley Forcum managed to get their six-shooters and emptied the shells from their chambers and handed them to Pete who surreptitiously slipped them into the chip bucket behind Chief's stove. "Mag" Jones and Gene Cooke finally got the two would-be combatants to bed and all forgot about the .45 shells innocently reposing in the chip bucket.

Early the next morning Chief got up to build his fire. By the dim lamp light he failed to see the deadly missiles among his starting fuel. When the fireworks started all the cowboys thought it was an Indian attack and there hadn't been an Indian scare on Eagle Creek in forty years.

One stove lid blew off and broke a window and another almost hit the cook when it flew into the air. The stove pipe fell over and the room filled with acrid smoke. Soot and ashes were everywhere. A pot of beans, left on the back of the stove, fell off and the cook slipped in the mess and banged his knee on the oven door which blew off. The shells, as each exploded, sounded like cannons and the cowboys began running into the kitchen, their baggy underwear flapping.

When the fireworks was over the kitchen was a shambles. It took the cowboys most of the day to clean the mess up and repair damages. And them with heads big enough to eat hay with the horses.

The cook told them in no uncertain terms what he thought of anyone that would slip .45 shells in his fuel. He never would believe it was anything but a vicious prank thought up by damnfool cowboys.

Rx for Man and Horse

Most roundup cooks were willing to share their precious kerosene, or "coal oil," with the cowboys for medicinal purposes. Plain old ordinary coal oil was used for flesh cuts, be it on man or horse, and it was known to be excellent for croup, taken with a spoon of sugar. Rubbed on strained muscles or bruises, it was beneficial in relieving pain. It was used for burns, scalds, and sores, for head lice, and for mange on horses.

Besides kerosene, the cook usually had a bottle of Sloans Liniment, and a can of Bickmore Salve, along with the vanilla and can of cinnamon. Somewhere in his gear would be a bottle of Gumbalts Caustic Balsam, and any cook worth the title would have a box of Epsom Salts and a bottle of castor oil. With doctors many miles from camp, a man had to treat his own aches and pains. The cook usually was custodian of the medicine chest.

Home remedies were much more commonly used than prescription medicines. Vinegar was used for "hick-ups," or hiccough. A few drops of strong vinegar on a small lump of sugar, and held in the mouth until dissolved, would stop most cases of hiccough. Vinegar was also used with either hot or cold water as a convenient stimulant for sprains and bruises, and a refreshing antiseptic for sponging the body in fever. It was also employed in the cure of ringworms, scab, and mange.

A beef's gall, mixed into a pint of alcohol, and bathed with frequently, was good for a weak back. Beef's gall was also useful in making a cleaning compound.

Baking soda was an old standby, and any roundup cook would have a supply. It was used for relieving sour stomach, heartburn,

[83]

water-brash, and was known to relieve diarrhea, or sudden distress of the stomach. A teaspoonful of soda was stirred into a wineglassful of water, and taken in one dose. It was also used for relief of wasp stings, ant or bee stings, and was used for rash or any kind of itch. A paste was made by dampening with just enough water to make a thin paste, and applied to the affected parts.

Tobacco was used as an aid to relieving the bites of insects, scorpions, and spiders. A wad of chewing tobacco applied to a fresh cut was considered the ultimate in first aid on the open range. Besides, it was almost always at hand, moist and warm from the mouth of the nearest tobacco-chewing cowboy.

Plain old common table salt was used in a dozen different ways. Heated dry, and put into a bag, it was applied to the outer surface of any inflammation, be it toothache, earache or stomach cramps. Gargling warm water and salt was good for catarrh and sore throat. Salt and cold water was good for sore or bleeding gums. A pinch of salt in hot water, taken before eating, aided digestion. It was considered a cure for dyspepsia. A cup of hot water and salt would quiet the severest case of vomiting when nothing else would. Browned or baked salt, mixed with a quart of water, was one of the best remedies for colic in horses. Infected wounds were often cured by soaking in salted hot water. For hay fever and other diseases that produced sneezing, a remedy that was quickly effective and often curative, was salt in hot vinegar. The patient would breathe the vapor for ten minutes at a time, four or five times a day.

Cinnamon was known to relieve vomiting, colic and diarrhea. A drop of cinnamon oil was used to relieve serious toothache.

Hops were known to have soothing and sleep-producing properties. The old-time cowboys were seldom bothered with insomnia. Their main worry was to find enough hours in a short night to sleep.

Dry tobacco was a valuable remedy for the cure of ascarides in horses. A diluted solution of tobacco thrown into the rectum of horses proved fatal to any worms found there. Used externally, it cured the mange in horses and dogs, and scabs in sheep. It was fatal to lice, fleas and ticks. For external applications, or for an enema in horses, an infusion was made by boiling one drachma of tobacco with a pint of water.

Boiled rice water was the most common remedy for diarrhea, and was the easiest obtainable, as almost all ranch kitchens kept a supply of rice, and a chuck box was not considered adequate without rice to make the delicious desert called "spotted pup."

Browned flour was another remedy used for relief of diarrhea. The well-scorched flour was mixed with boiled water, or milk, and given as a drink. This was considered the best remedy for scours in calves and foals.

The early day cowboys were a tough and rugged species. They had to be. The only time one went to a doctor was for severely broken bones, or possibly, a case of blood poisoning. Minor breaks, such as a fractured finger, toe, or even cracked ribs, could be tolerated while carrying on partial duties.

From an old diary, over a hundred years old, comes a tale of sickness and endurance. A man by the name of Johnson, in the early spring of 1866, put together a herd of longhorn steers, over a thousand head, near Goliad, Texas. He intended to trail to Sedalia, Missouri, at that time a railhead.

Johnson recruited his trail crew from the hordes of returning Civil War veterans. These boys and young men had only recently exchanged their cavalry saddle for the cowboy saddle and wore their army guns with a nonchalant ease gained through practice. They were lanky tow-headed boys that four years of war had not embittered. With exuberant whoops and rebel yells they strung the herd out on a trail into country they had never seen. Had there been a more adequate chronicler than Johnson, an epic could have been written. At that, he appeared to be an educated man.

His diary states briefly, on April 1, 1866, "Camped on Red River . . . some boys taken sick." Several days elapse before the boys' ailment is mentioned again. Stampedes, after leaving Colbert's Ferry, and the days spent in rounding up the scattered cattle took up Johnson's diary space. But, a week later Johnson again comments: "Seven men now so sick they cannot set the saddle. Jobe [a mix-breed of Cherokee Indian and Negro, who was cook] has two riding on his cart. Jobe cooked three sage hens for soup. Men have High fever and Diarrhea. All have terrible chills. Jobe made oak bark tea."

A person can only imagine how the boy trail drivers suffered under such adverse conditions and lack of comforts. Riding nightguard in the chill April, sleeping on the ground with only a few "hen-skins" for covering, the youths seldom undressed, merely removing hat and boots on retiring. They spent from twelve to fourteen grueling hours in the saddle which must have been almost unendurable. When again Johnson tells of the plight of his youthful crew, he says, "Laid over a week for men to recuperate." By this time Johnson's herd was passing over the lands of the Five Civilized Nations of Indians. Jobe, being half Cherokee, was a member of one of these tribes. Even though other outfits crossing cattle through the land of the Five Nations ran into trouble that year, Johnson, through Jobe's intercession, paid ten cents per head, and grazed his herd on the lush prairie.

While holding the herd in this area Johnson wrote, "Eddie Grimes died from the fever and we buried him yesterday on the prairie. Rain and cold has been bad for all." Johnson himself came down with the mysterious fever, and suffered violent chills for two days while driving the herd in a constant downpour. Jobe seems to be the only person on the drive who escaped the malady.

A week later Johnson wrote, "We left Jack Smith with Indians as he was too weak to ride. He cried and begged to be tied to his saddle. We all owe our lives to Jobe and his Herbs and Medicines."

Weeks later, the herd reached Baxter Springs in the southeastern corner of Kansas, then on northeast to Sedalia, Missouri. Johnson commented briefly on the health of his cattle and then his men. "Cattle in good shape. Men hale and hearty." Shortly after, Johnson sold his cattle, and his trail driver's diary states briefly: "Heading for home."

In 1873, a cook by the name of McSplan was lord of the pots and pans for a trail herd heading up the northern trail out of Texas. Somewhere along the route, McSplan was bitten by a diamondback rattlesnake. Not just once, but twice, by the same snake. The story goes that McSplan, reaching for some provender under the chuck wagon, put his hand on the snake and was bitten on the index finger. In his wrath at being bitten, McSplan grabbed a shovel and began stabbing and gouging at the reptile. In his frenzy, the cook became careless, and was bitten again on the back of the wrist. "No whiskey on the wagon" evidently was the rule in this case because McSplan put his hand in a pan of kerosene and salt as a cure. For several hours following the snakebites, McSplan suffered several spasms, and had the utmost difficulty in breathing. However, the next day McSplan was back slinging his dutch ovens, and little the worse for his experience — outside of a swollen hand. Later, it was to cause such an irritating itch that McSplan complained of losing sleep.

Grady Lee, as a young cowboy staying in a lone line-riders' camp in the Panhandle, in the winter of 1918, suffered a severe case of the flu. Miles from the nearest neighbor, and chances of a passer-by slim — Grady suffered for ten days, half of the time in delirium. His supplies were low, but he had flour and a supply of fresh beef. Two boxes of dry mustard in his cupboard, along with a jug of vinegar, were the only commodities that could even faintly be termed medicinal. From the mustard and vinegar, the young cowboy made a paste and spread it on a strip of blanket. Heated, this was placed over his chest and back. He subsisted entirely on beef broth, as his throat became so inflamed he could barely swallow. Kerosene, used for his lamp, was also in short supply. He used the remaining oil, mixed with tallow, for further poultices, and a few drops diluted in warm water as a gargle. After ten days he rode eighteen miles to the home ranch for fresh supplies, and returned to his lonely camp the following day.

In the early days, a good well-trained horse was harder to come by than were cowboys, and received better care in many instances. A late-nineties veterinary book gives a remedy for horse colic:

"Two ounces of laudanum, one-half ounce spirits of camphor — or one gram gum camphor, two ounces spirits of niter, two drams fluid extract belladonna. Mix with one-half pint water, and give as a drench. If the horse is no better in one hour, repeat, and if constipated, use warm water injections. These prescriptions are equally good for man; a relatively less quantity is to be given, of course." [Of course!] "A good dose of hot whiskey and water, if nothing else is at hand, would be in the right direction." Well, why didn't they say so in the first place! Few, if any, cowcamps were without some whiskey, and whiskey could be used for any internal ailment known under the sun — be it for man or beast.

One time, years ago, I related to an old Apache friend a recipe of my own, used with great success as a cough syrup. I described the correct amounts of honey, mixed with lemon juice, whiskey, and melted butter. I said it was good, and that kids like it. The old man's eyes crinkled, and he said, "Of course it was good. *Anything* with whiskey in it is good."

PART II

Recipes

Deep Pit Barbecue

There are several ways to barbecue meat, but if you perfect this one method you don't need to know any other. However, if you like your barbecue with lots of crust, half charred, and pungently smoked, you won't like my method so you can simply skip this chapter.

For barbecuing one-half beef, or two hundred and fifty pounds, dig a hole four feet deep, three feet wide, and six or seven feet long. Select your site for the pit with care. Stay away from low ground and sandy or gravelly soil. Keep the pit away from large trees in order to avoid troublesome roots. And remember, the fire will scorch leaves of nearby trees if the pit is too close. If you dig the pit several days ahead you can keep it dry by covering with tin, or a tarp, or sheets of heavy plastic. Whatever you do, don't let the pit get wet.

Now for the wood. If you don't have an abundance of good dry hardwood, forget it! You can't barbecue with resinous wood such as pine, spruce, fir, cedar, juniper, or piñon. Nor can you have success with aspen, poplar, cottonwood, or willow.

So get about a cord of oak or hickory. If you are lucky enough to live in the Southwest, use mesquite. Some fruit woods are OK — such as well-cured apple and cherry. I've been told alder and ash make good barbecue coals, but if I don't have a good supply of oak or mesquite I refuse to do *any* barbecuing.

You have to start the fire in the pit at least five hours before putting in the meat. Six or seven hours burning time doesn't hurt. Don't fill the pit chock full of wood at first, but burn a layer of logs, and when they are nice red coals add another layer of wood. Just remember it's impossible to have too many coals but it's a major disaster if you don't have enough.

[91]

I witnessed a catastrophe once, and I'll tell about it so it may serve as a grim warning to anyone that thinks he can skimp on wood or use a damp pit.

A cattlemen's group, preparing for a grand feed, dug a pit near a creek bed. The weather had been unusually wet and the pit was damp. Very damp. I think if they'd dug a foot deeper they'd have struck water. Anyhow, they decided the fire would dry the pit out. They ran into more trouble when they didn't have an adequate supply of good dry oak. Some of the wood was too green, and most of it was damp. A good part of it was logs too large for the purpose. The men simply hoped for the best, as cowmen are extremely optimistic (or they couldn't stay in the cattle business). So they went ahead and put in a hundred and fifty pounds of prime beef all seasoned and wrapped. They covered the meat with corrugated tin and filled the pit with dirt and forgot about it until one o'clock the next day.

Two hundred hungry people watched the uncovering of the pit. The first packet of meat ran red, red. A murmur of dismay rippled through the crowd when all the meat was discovered to be too rare to eat. The indomitable cooks found an old bed spring, built another fire above ground, and spent two hours turning chunks of meat over the flames. By three o'clock the starving crowd was fed some well-smoked, hard-crusted barbecue.

Now, I wouldn't want this to happen to my worst enemy, so let's get back to the fire building.

After you have some eighteen inches of good red coals, remove any charred chunks of wood that may not have burned completely. A pitchfork or long-handled shovel can be used for this purpose. If you've used the proper wood there won't be any unburned logs to remove.

When there are no longer any flames you can lay down a strip of tin directly on the coals. The tin must be just slightly more narrow than the pit. Or two pieces of tin can be used, overlapping them. Don't put in the tin until the moment you are ready to put in the meat.

This is the way to prepare the meat.

Cut roasts of beef, using front quarters, hind quarters, ribs, neck — all except the T-bones, which you'll want to save for grilling. No need to trim away the fat, nor do you need to bone the

WIRE LOOP
FOR EASY
HANDLING

MEAT WRAPPED IN FOIL, THEN IN
BURLAP SACK, TIED WITH WIRE,
READY FOR THE PIT.
15 Pound Roast

BALING WIRE
ATTACHED TO TIN

DIRT — FIRMLY PACKED —
NO AIR HOLES

CORREGATED TIN

MEAT

CORREGATED TIN

PIT IS
4' DEEP

18" HARDWOOD COALS

3' WIDE

BURN HARDWOOD 5 TO 7 HOURS.
WRAP 12 TO 15 POUND ROASTS.
MINIMUM TIME 7½ HOURS.
CAN BE LEFT IN PIT 10 TO 12 HOURS.
MEAT MUST BE THAWED BEFORE WRAPPING.
USE WIRE CUTTERS WHEN OPENING BUNDLES
JUST PRIOR TO SERVING.

roasts. Just be sure the meat is not frozen. Cuts should weigh about fifteen pounds and not less than ten. Flavor them any way you like, but I go a little wild and scatter thick slices of onion, slivers of fresh garlic, and some crumpled bay leaf. I use fresh ground pepper and salt. Sprinkle on plenty of monosodium glutamate and several dashes of liquid smoke. Go easy on the smoke — just a hint will do.

Now, each roast must be wrapped well in extra heavy foil. Or stockinet or toweling will do. I think the foil helps retain the juices best and is easier to handle later when taken from the pit.

Put foil-wrapped meat into a gunny sack (burlap feed bag), fold over until it is a tight bundle, and tie with wire. Baling wire or "stay" wire serves best. Leave a twist or handle in the center of the bundle so removing from the pit can be done by hooking a gonch-hook onto the handle. Wet the sacks. They don't need to be sopping wet, just run a hose over them lightly or dip them briefly in a tub of water.

Now the meat is ready for the pit. Put the bundles of meat in quickly. Arrange them a few inches apart or merely touching. Don't pile them on top of each other. Lay a strip of tin over meat, being sure all the bundles are covered. Then begin filling the pit with dirt, making sure no dirt touches the bags of meat. Several shovelers can cover the meat in a few minutes. Be sure no air pockets remain. Check later, and if even a wisp of smoke is escaping add more dirt.

The meat takes seven to eight hours to cook. Leaving it in the pit longer doesn't hurt. Often I leave it for ten to twelve hours and dig it out just prior to serving the meal. The very minimum length of time is seven hours for twelve to fifteen pound roasts. If you like pink or rare barbecue you can remove the meat in slightly less than seven hours.

In barbecuing beef for 2,500 Apaches at San Carlos in 1972, we dug the pit by backhoe machine. It was thirty feet long by three feet wide by four feet deep. We used 1,600 pounds of beef with bone intact. We used the entire beef except for some neck meat I used for making stock for barbecue sauce. We burned almost two cords of mesquite wood cut in four-foot lengths. The fire burned for seven hours before we put in the bundles of meat. The meat remained in the pit for eleven hours.

The barbecue was served at high noon and no one went home hungry. Now, I expect to hear cries of "No rocks? You can't barbecue meat without lining the pit with boulders!" Well, the heck I can't. I've been doing it my way for years and I've never used rocks yet. The only time I can see any sense in using rocks is if the pit is wet. Hauling a bunch of rocks is sweating, hard work. And unless you're a slave owner I can't see any earthly reason for going to all that trouble.

Down in south Texas they have a method of barbecuing beef over pits of coals, meat lying on racks or heavy wire mesh. The cooks sweat over this furnace, turning the meat and swabbing on the sauce with mops. Maybe labor is cheap in Texas so they can be forgiven for going to all that work. Their method makes fine eating — I have no quarrel with that, but my way of deep pit barbecuing is so darned easy on the cook. You can devote the leisure time to doing more exciting things, such as attending the prebarbecue cocktail party or perhaps taking a long siesta.

We musn't forget the modern housewife, say from Chicago, who doesn't mind a small hole dug in her lawn. She can barbecue delicious meat right in her own backyard.

A twenty-pound turkey, stuffed and foil wrapped, can be roasted in a pit as small as three by three by three. Burn hardwood (where local open fire law permits) about four hours, lay down the tin, put in gunnysack-wrapped turkey the same as for beef barbecue. Cover with another sheet of tin and fill pit with dirt. Soil, well packed, should be twelve to fourteen inches deep. The bird will take ten to twelve hours to cook. Be sure the fowl is well thawed before wrapping.

Dutch Oven Cookery

Preparing a meal in dutch ovens should not be attempted without a little foreknowledge of the sheer mechanics in the art of dutch oven cookery.

So we'll start at the beginning with a description of a dutch oven. The standard pattern has not changed since pioneer days. The manufacture of the oven originally was in England but the Hollanders brought such large quantities for trade in America it was soon called a "Dutch" oven.

If the dutch oven does not have three stubby legs and if it is not made of heavy cast iron it is not a real dutch oven. The lid is slightly domed and made of the same heavy metal with a small handle so it may be lifted with a gonch hook, and has a two-inch flange for holding coals. The oven itself has a sturdy free-swinging bail.

The most common sizes range from the tiny "two-serving" eight inch oven to the large sixteen inchers. Ovens with shallow sides of about four inches are called "bread" ovens and the much deeper ones with a depth of eight to ten inches are meat ovens. Some modern, so-called camp ovens, without legs and domed glass lids found in sporting goods stores, are for cooking on a modern range and are *not for baking on coals from a campfire*.

You can't find a dutch oven for sale in your supermarket or local sporting goods store. Trading posts in the western United States still carry them, and if not, most will order one for you from their wholesale supplier. Good old-fashioned hardware stores in the Southwest are good bets for locating one.

Now that you know what a dutch oven looks like we'll start with the next most important thing, and that is the proper kind of fire. For an hour, and not one minute less, build your fire with good hardwood — and don't be stingy! There's nothing as frustrating as lack of enough coals when you are ready to begin cooking. Especially

WARM DUTCH OVEN—
ADD GREASE AND START
PINCHING OFF BISCUITS
AND CROWD 'EM IN
UNTIL BOTTOM IS COVERED

USE ONLY HARDWOOD COALS—
OAK OR MESQUITE. SOFT WOOD
SUCH AS PINE, CEDAR, JUNIPER OR
COTTONWOOD WILL NOT MAKE
PROPER COALS FOR BAKING.

PRE-HEAT LID— EVENLY—
HOT, BUT NOT RED-HOT.

SET OVEN ON LEVEL BED OF
COALS (LIVE AND RED). PILE UP
ALONG SIDES OF OVEN.
THEN PUT ON HOT LID AND FILL
TO RIM WITH HOT COALS.

WHEN PEEKIN', BE
CAREFUL NOT TO SPILL
ASHES ON BISCUITS.

WHILE BAKING, LIFT ENTIRE
DUTCH OVEN AND ROTATE BY
QUARTER TURNS TO ASSURE
COOKING EVENLY —

LIFT LID
AND ROTATE
SEVERAL TIMES

IF BISCUITS BROWN
FASTER ON TOP — REMOVE LID,
DUMP COALS, PUT LID BACK
ON OVEN.
IF BISCUITS BROWN TOO FAST
ON THE BOTTOM REMOVE OVEN
FROM COALS. BISCUITS WILL
FINISH BAKING IN HOT OVEN.

STELLA HUGHES

when baking bread. So pile on the mesquite or oak, both excellent woods for making fine coals. (There are other hardwoods such as ironwood, hickory, maple and alder.) Whatever you do don't try to use soft woods such as pine, juniper, cedar, spruce, cottonwood or aspen. At least, if you intend to bake bread. You can fry foods with soft resinous woods but none will hold heat or make good hot coals for baking in dutch ovens. About all a conifer log is good for is its pungent odor and an abundance of miserable black smoke. It does make a fine "bull" fire in the evenings to set around and spin yarns.

I like to build my fire in a "fire hole" — probably because I learned to do my outdoor cooking in the windy part of northern Arizona, where a person soon learns, if they build their fire flat on the ground, it's liable to be in the next county by the time you have your biscuits ready for the oven. So I do as the San Carlos Apaches do, dig a hole four or five feet in length and one and a half feet deep. I slant the front to the back and use two iron pipes (two-inch serves best) laid lengthwise for fire irons. I block the ends so the pipe does not roll, and on these rods go the dutch ovens and lids for heating. Very little cooking is done on the open flame. We use coals to cook with and these are scooped from the fire hole with a flat bottomed shovel and put to one side. Arranged in neat piles just slightly larger than your oven you can have as many "stoves" as you have piles of coals.

While your fire is burning down so you have a good supply of coals you can mix your biscuits. Meanwhile put both the dutch oven and lid on the fire irons to heat. The oven should be just warm, but the lid must remain until it is hot. But not red hot. Remove warm oven, brush generously with grease, both bottom and sides. Oven should be warm enough to melt grease slowly. If it hisses and smokes it's too derned hot! Let it cool a little before you crowd in your biscuits. Put hot lid on at once.

From the fire take at least two shovels of good coals. Put them off to one side so you won't be stepping in them. Break up the larger coals to walnut size or slightly bigger. Arrange them evenly on the ground and put the dutch oven squarely on them. Try to make oven as level as possible. Then place good live coals on the lid, filling to the brim of the flange. These too should be broken up and distributed as evenly as possible. If the wind is blowing you will have to watch closely or the coals will get too hot. You can tone the hot

STACKED DUTCH OVENS —
SAVES COALS.

A 16" DUTCH OVEN USED FOR BAKING
BISCUITS SHOULD BE ONLY 4½" DEEP.
OVENS 6" OR 7" DEEP ARE CALLED MEAT OVENS
AND ARE BEST SUITED FOR ROASTS OR STEWS.

A 16" BREAD OVEN WILL HOLD 32
TO 35 BISCUITS.

IRON PIPES USED FOR
FIRE IRONS — TRENCH FOR
COALS. USE DIRT TO KEEP
PIPES FROM ROLLING OFF ROCKS.

STELLA HUGHES

coals down a bit by adding ashes, but don't kill your heat by putting on too many ashes at once.

Now, you set back and have your second cup of coffee; unless you are a worrywart. In that case you will be peeking at the baking bread every minute or so. Try not to do this, as each time you sneak a peep you are letting the heat out and cold air in. When lifting the lid with the gonch hook be sure to lift straight up so that lid does not tilt and spill ashes onto the bread. If a few ashes do fall in, no great tragedy. They really don't taste so bad and can be brushed off after the bread is done.

After the bread has been cooking for six to ten minutes take the gonch hook, and by the bail, lift the entire dutch oven, lid and all, and rotate it by quarter turns on the coals. Then lift the lid carefully and give it quarter turns. This assures biscuits baking evenly. There will naturally be a few hot spots. If coals are far too hot on one side, remove oven and take your shovel and rearrange coals evenly. If biscuits brown too fast on top, remove lid, dump ashes and return lid to oven at once.

When bread looks done, test by taking a fork and gently lifting a biscuit from the center. If it looks thoroughly baked and top and bottom is a golden brown, remove from coals at once. You can move lid a few inches off center so bread will not "sweat," or biscuits can be removed from oven and put in a pan to keep warm and the oven used to fry bacon and eggs. However, if you are an old "pro" you'll have bacon and eggs ready just as the biscuits are done and can yell "come and git it or I'll throw it to the mangey coyotes."

My sister, Verena Beasley, when she was first learning to cook with dutch ovens, tells of the time she tried to bake biscuits with aspen coals. Now, I can't think of a more unsuitable wood, but she was green as a gourd, so didn't know any better.

"It was up at the old Huey Bar place on the Mountain," Verena explains. "The only kind of wood available was pine, spruce and aspen. Well, aspen was the easiest to chop so that's what I used."

The "Mountain," I might add, was the Mogollon Rim south of Winslow, Arizona, and Verena was camped alone at the old abandoned ranch while her husband Roy was working as a fire guard for the Forest Service. As she was a bride and a novice she can be forgiven for her ignorance.

Verena goes on to tell of her traumatic experience.

"I didn't even have enough sense to pre-heat the oven and lid. Instead I put the biscuits in the cold oven and set it on the aspen coals and settled back to watch my first batch of dutch oven biscuits bake. Nothing happened. So I piled on more coals. Still no action. So I put another big shovel full under the oven and a whole lot more on top. After an hour the biscuits looked like cement disks. Then something happened all right! I had a screaming fit! It was O.K. though, as there wasn't a human being within ten miles. I tossed the cement missiles into the nearby forest and even the blue jays couldn't make a dent in them."

Since that long ago "trial by fire" Verena became an excellent camp cook and I doubt if there is anything she can't cook to perfection on a dutch oven. On one occasion I saw her turn out a lemon pie, with meringue topping browned to a golden hue. Anyone eating this pie would have sworn it had been baked on a modern gas range.

Verena can bake cookies and cakes, either in the bottom of the oven or in a pan and placed on rocks in the oven. She bakes custards and puddings by burying the oven in hot ashes. Stews, roasts or deep-dish cobblers can all be buried in hot coals. All kinds of fish and fowl are roasted by placing a small amount of water in the oven and letting them do their own basting. In other words, any dish can be cooked in a dutch oven; all a person needs is the savvy or know-how. So get a dutch oven and have fun.

A Note About How To Find Chili and Avoid That Other Stuff

Naturally, many Southwestern dishes call for chili — and it's worth the trouble to find the real thing. The long green Anaheim chili when fresh, roasted, and peeled is used for making chili rellenos — or chopped and soaked in vinegar and used on frijoles. This chili is harvested in late summer and is ready for picking when nice and solid, dark green, and from six to eight inches long. It is kept fresh under refrigeration or roasted and peeled and frozen. It is dried by hanging in full sun and when crisp and a brilliant red in color is ready for storing in a dry place for winter or for years. Various companies such as Ortega, Ashlys, and Hunts, put it up in cans.

The best chili for making Mexican food is Santa Cruz brand packaged in boxes and put out by Santa Cruz Chili Company at Amado, Arizona. This is a coarse ground chili made from good red chilies. You can get it mild, *picante* (hot), or, if you ask, a grind for sausage makers that is a little hotter than hot. Now such chili is not to be confused with the horrible stuff put out by many of the national spice labels. These companies grind up a little red chili powder, and add paprika, cumin, salt, oregano, red pepper, garlic powder, marjoram, nutmeg, allspice, sawdust and horse manure.

El Pato is a brand of chili sauce we use all the time on the roundups. It's sorta hot but the Indians like it on frijoles and meat. We hire a number of Mexicans and of course they use it on everything but the rice pudding.

Jalapeños aren't for human consumption. They are used to start charcoal fires — seriously, they are to be used sparingly when a recipe calls for chili.

Kitchen Weights and Measurements

4 even saltspoons ....1 teaspoon
4 teaspoonfuls ....1 tablespoon
4 tablespoonfuls ....1 wineglass or ¼ cup
8 tablespoonfuls ....½ cup or 1 gill
2 gills or 1 cup ....½ pint
4 gills or 2 cups ....1 pint
2 pints ....1 quart
4 quarts ....1 gallon
1 even tablespoonful lard ....1 ounce
1 heaping tablespoonful lard ....2 ounces
Butter or lard size of walnut ....1 ounce
1 even cupful of butter ....½ pound
4 cupfuls flour ....1 quart or 1 pound
3 cupfuls cornmeal ....1 pound
2 cupfuls granulated sugar ....1 pound
2½ cupfuls powdered sugar ....1 pound

Meat

How To Keep Fresh Meat in Summer

In the summer time you can keep fresh meat nicely for a week or two, like farmers or ranchers do, by putting it into sour milk or buttermilk and placing it in a cool cellar. The bone or fat need not be removed. Rinse well when ready to use.

In the Southwest, where nights are apt to be cool and days hot, meat can be kept ten days to two weeks, if hung out after dark, where the night breeze hits meat fully. Meat can be hung in a tree or screened meathouse, brought in at the crack of dawn, and wrapped very well in canvas or tarps, and stored during the day in as cool a place as can be found. Under the bed of the chuck wagon is an ideal place. Just be sure sun does not hit the wrapped meat. The night coolness must be retained in meat all day.

When using during the day for cooking, take out only meat needed for meal and quickly wrap meat again. Be sure blow flies do not get to deposit eggs on meat.

If it rains on the meat at night, it will surely spoil. Any meat that sours from damp weather is ruined. Meat that has been rained on or out in muggy and damp nights will have to be either cooked at once or jerked.

Putting Down Beef for Winter

Cut your beef into sizable pieces, sprinkle a little salt upon bottom of barrel, then pack your beef without salt amongst it, and when packed, pour over it a brine made by dissolving 6 pounds of salt for each 100 pounds of meat in just sufficient cold water to handsomely cover it.

Or for each 100 pounds of beef cut up in sizable chunks, use 5 pounds of salt, ¼ ounce saltpeter, 1 pound of brown sugar; dissolve in sufficient water to cover meat; 2 weeks after take up, drain, throw away brine, make more the same as first. It will keep the season through. When boiled for eating, put into boiling water; for soups into cold water.

How To Make Jerky

The Spanish word for dried beef is "Charqui," and we call it jerky. To dry beef, cut meat in strips as long as 6 to 14 inches. No wider than 1 inch is best so that meat will dry quickly. Do not leave fat on meat as it becomes rancid in a short time. Cut against grain where at all possible. Sprinkle each piece of meat with salt and pepper; and if so inclined, a small amount of powdered chili.

Hang strips of meat in a dry place on wire lines. Full sun is not necessary, but is best. A shed or barn loft will do. Cellars and basements are not at all suitable as they are too damp. The clothesline is fine if it does not rain. Do not worry about flies as the salt and pepper repels them. In very hot weather meat will be jerked in a few days or a week. Just be sure meat does not get wet. When meat looks and feels like old shoe leather, remove from drying wires and store in flour sacks in a cool place. Hanging from rafters by thin wires keeps weevils, mice, and other pests away.

— *Clair Haight, Hashknife Outfit, Winslow, Arizona, 1922*

Jerky Gravy

Take a quart of jerky and pound each piece into flakes and powder. An anvil or sad iron makes a good pounding base. Use heavy wooden mallet or hammer. Remove any dry fiber or rancid fat. Put pounded meat in hot dutch oven with 2 or 3 tablespoons bacon drippings. When mixed well stir in several spoons flour, let brown, then pour correct amount of milk slowly, stirring constantly so there will be no lumps. This gravy will probably not need seasoning as jerky will have retained its salt and pepper. Serve on hot dutch oven biscuits, or on plain boiled potatoes with jackets. Jerky gravy is good on boiled rice, macaroni, or mashed potatoes.

— *Clair Haight, Hashknife Outfit, Winslow, Arizona, 1922*

Spiced Corned Beef

To 10 pounds of beef, take 2 cups salt, 2 cups molasses, 2 tablespoonfuls saltpeter, 1 tablespoonful ground pepper, 1 table-spoonful cloves; rub well into the beef. Turn every day, and rub the mixture in. Will be ready for use in 10 days.

— "Barney" Borneman, Eagle Creek, Arizona

Home Corned Beef

10   pounds lean beef (no bone)
 8   quarts cold water
 1   oz. sodium nitrate
 2   tablespoons brown sugar
 1   tablespoon mixed whole spices
20   bay leaves
 8   to 10 cloves garlic

Combine all ingredients except meat and boil ten minutes. Place meat in crock fitted with tight lid. Pour pickling solution over meat as soon as it is cold. Then weigh meat down with a rock or wooden board which fits inside crock. Cover top with cloth. Store in cool place for two weeks.

— "Barney" Borneman, Eagle Creek, Arizona

Canned Beef

You can make a good stew out of canned roast beef or corned beef when you are in camp and out of fresh meat. Cut your vegetables in small squares and brown them in ham or bacon fat. I cook the carrots, turnips, potatoes, and onions nearly done, then add my tomatoes and canned meat last. Let cook a few minutes and thicken with flour made smooth in a little water. You can put baking powder biscuits on top. Put in oven if cooking on a stove. If in camp put hot coals on dutch oven lid and bake until biscuits are golden brown. Do not use coals under oven as stew will scorch.

— Herb Nichols, Clifton, Arizona

Son-of-a-bitch Stew
(Son-of-a-gun or S.O.B.)

To be made the eve of butchering or the day after.

Put in hot dutch oven enough lard or bacon drippings to cover bottom about ¼ inch deep. Cut up all of marrow gut from one young beef into one-inch pieces. Put in hot fat and brown. This takes at least a half hour. Meanwhile you'll be busy. Dice up all the heart. Discard unsuitable trimmings. Use only good part. Dice all the sweetbreads, both kidneys, about a pound of butcher steak (neck meat or flank will do fine). Now add all this to browned marrow guts. Continue frying. After about a half hour add about a fourth of liver diced into very small pieces. Peel two large onions and dice. Add to mixture. Add several cloves garlic. Don't be afraid to put in plenty of garlic; after what all else has gone in, a little garlic can't hurt. Salt and pepper to taste. By this time the whole mess might start to become too brown or to stick and it's time to add water. Cook and cook and cook. It will take most of day slow simmering to be done. Keep adding water as needed. Stew must be very done or marrow guts will be tough and rubbery. Now here are some variations:

Add chili powder if desired.

Two or three pounds diced potatoes may be added about a half hour before stew is done.

This amount will serve ten or twelve hungry cowboys.

— *Allen Hardt, Double Circle Ranch, Eagle Creek, Arizona*

Beef Guts

Take beef guts (the last four or five feet are the tenderest) strip out the green stuff. Wash thoroughly and turn wrong side out with a stick or broom handle. Wipe dry. Cut into pieces 3 or 4 inches long. Place in pan and roast in oven over medium heat until tender. Or place in broiler, salt and pepper and use a little monosodium glutamate if you have it. Sweetbreads, slices of heart, and kidney may be roasted along with beef guts at the same time. The guts take longer to cook.

Pickled Tongue

Take a beef tongue, wash in cold water and put in large kettle, fill with water and boil until done. This takes from 3 to 4 hours. Be sure tongue is fully cooked by piercing with fork. Plunge tongue into cold water, and after 5 to 10 minutes remove and let cool on towel. Peel skin from tongue and slice. Put in jar large enough to hold with about 2 inches of space at top. Cover with a solution made of half vinegar and half water. Add ½ cup of sugar, and salt and pepper to taste. Dice 1 clove of garlic, and add slices of raw onion. Sweet pickle juice added to vinegar solution is good. Store in refrigerator at least 12 hours before serving.

— Stella Hughes

Mountain Oysters

Mountain oysters are obtained twice during the year — spring and fall roundup when the bull calves are castrated. Very young calves (only a few weeks old) are too small, and the ones taken from long yearlin's are too large and strong tasting.

As soon as the pail of oysters are brought in from the branding, wash them in cold water. Then put in fresh water with 1 cup salt to soak for awhile. Drain and wipe dry. Slit lengthwise of oyster and cut off tips. Peel off skin and if of fair size slit lengthwise. Salt and pepper and roll in flour. Fry in fat as you would frying chicken. Be sure oysters are well done and crisp. Serve hot with potatoes and green salad. Waldorf salad or cabbage salad is good with Mountain Oysters.

— Chief Maybre, Double Circle Ranch, Eagle Creek, Arizona

Dutch Oven Swiss Steak

3 pounds round steak at least one inch thick
½ cup flour
2 tablespoonfuls fat
salt and pepper
boiling water
bit of bay leaf if desired

Pound the steak until the fiber is thoroughly broken up; add the flour with salt and pepper while pounding. When the steak is tender, the flour should be thoroughly absorbed into the steaks. Melt fat in dutch oven; put in the meat and let brown on one side, then turn and brown on the other side. Add boiling water and let simmer until tender. Maybe as much as two hours or more. The bay leaf, if used, should be crumbled and added with the water.

Veal Loaf

Chop fine or run through a meat mincer, 1½ pounds of veal steak. Add about 2 ounces of fat, salt pork or bacon; add 1 egg and the yolk of another, beaten light; one pimento chopped fine, a tablespoonful parsley chopped fine, ½ teaspoonful powdered thyme, 2 tablespoonfuls of thick cream or ¼ cup of sauce (cream tomato or similar sauce), ½ teaspoonful each of salt and paprika, a grating of nutmeg, and 2 crackers rolled fine; mix all together in a compact roll; set into a baking dish on a slice of salt pork, with a slice of pork above. Bake about 2 hours at 350 degrees, basting often with hot fat. Serve cold, sliced thin, with potatoes or green salads.

— *Ike Hawkins, Clifton, Arizona*

Pot Roast With Currants

Purchase at least 4 pounds of beef in a solid piece from chuck or round, roll the meat in flour. Have ready some hot salt pork fat, or fat from top of a kettle of soup, in a frying pan. In this, cook and turn the meat until it is seared and browned all over. Set the meat into a saucepan or iron kettle (the latter is the most suitable utensil), pour in a cup of boiling water, sprinkle over the meat ⅔ cup of dried currants, cover the kettle close, and let cook where the water will simply simmer very gently. Add water as needed, just enough to keep in the moisture. Dutch oven on campfire is perfect. It will take 5 or 6 hours. Cook until the meat is very tender. Remove the meat to a serving dish. Then stir into the liquid 2 tablespoons flour, salted to taste and smoothed in about ½ cup of cold water; stir until boiling, let simmer 10 minutes, then pour over meat. Serve with plain boiled potatoes, turnips, or squash and cabbage.

— Ike Hawkins, Clifton, Arizona

Dutch Oven Beef Loaf

¾ cup milk
1 egg
1½ cups bread crumbs (fine)
1 teaspoon salt
½ teaspoon oregano
1 small onion (finely minced)
1 cup catsup
2 pounds lean ground beef
1 tablespoon brown sugar
1 tablespoon worcestershire sauce

Combine milk, egg, bread crumbs, salt, oregano and onion with ground beef. Mix well. Pat into well-greased 12-inch dutch oven. Bake on medium to slow coals 1 hour. Combine catsup, brown sugar, and worcestershire sauce, bring to boil. Pour on beef loaf and bake 10 more minutes.

— Ike Hawkins, Clifton, Arizona

Cowboy Stew

2 pounds beef, cut in cubes
6 potatoes
6 carrots
1 cabbage
1 onion
salt and pepper to taste

Brown meat in dutch oven in bacon fat. Cover with water and simmer for 1 hour. After an hour, add carrots, salt, and pepper. 30 minutes later, add onion and potatoes. 30 minutes later, add cabbage and cook 15 minutes more. The broth may be thickened when done, if desired, by making a smooth paste of flour and water and adding to stew.

— Chief Maybre, Double Circle Ranch, Eagle Creek, Arizona

Shepherd's Beef Pie

Take 4 cups of cooked beef, cubed
about 2½ cups leftover gravy
2 or 3 cups leftover vegetables (potatoes, carrots, string beans,
        peas, etc.)
1 small onion, minced
parsley flakes
salt and pepper
3 cups hot mashed potatoes
1 egg, well beaten

Combine meat, gravy, vegetables, onion, parsley flakes, salt, and pepper. Heat to boiling point, stirring often. Put mixture in dutch oven or baking dish. Combine mashed potatoes and egg in bowl, mix thoroughly. Cover top of casserole or drop in spoonfuls. Bake in hot oven, 425 degrees, for 15 or 20 minutes or until brown.

— Herb Nichols, Clifton, Arizona

Spanish Beef Hash

1 cup cooked roast beef, chopped
4 cooked potatoes, diced
2 small onions, minced
½ cup green peppers, chopped (optional)
1 cup canned tomatoes
1 egg
1 can tomato sauce
garlic and chili powder to taste
salt and pepper as desired

Mix all ingredients, put in baking dish or dutch oven. Bake about 25 minutes.

— Herb Nichols, Clifton, Arizona

Beef Steak (Mexican Style)

Take boneless steaks about 6 or 8 ounces each. Pound 1 level teaspoon of Mexican chili powder into each steak. Season with salt and roll in cornmeal, pressing the meal into each beaten steak. Put bacon fat into large frying pan or dutch oven and let get hot. Place steaks in pan and fry until done. Mix 1 cup minced onions, 1 teaspoon minced garlic, 2 cups thick tomato sauce, 2 cups hot water, 1 teaspoon Mexican chili powder and salt to taste. Pour over steaks and simmer until onions are done. Serve steaks with sauce. Goes fine with rice or tortillas.

— Tom (Chili) Peppers, V Cross T Ranch, Magdelena, New Mexico

Liver Patties

1 pound beef liver
1 small onion, chopped fine
1 egg, beaten
3 tablespoons bacon fat
2 slices bacon
3 tablespoons flour

In a frying pan fry bacon until crisp, remove and break into small bits.

Put liver through meat grinder, using large blade. Add onion, flour, egg and bacon pieces. Mix well. Salt and pepper to taste.

Put bacon fat in skillet and heat. Drop liver by tablespoonfuls into fat and cook about 1½ minutes on each side.

— *Ike Hawkins, Clifton, Arizona*

Macaroni and Beef

Boil one pound of macaroni in rapidly boiling, salted water until tender; drain well.

In dutch oven add two tablespoonfuls of bacon fat; one large chopped onion, fry until slightly browned. Add 2 or 3 cups chopped leftover roast or steak and one cup meat stock. Add 2 cups canned tomatoes (well drained) or thick tomato puree. Add the cooked macaroni, salt and pepper and simmer slowly for about twenty minutes.

Beef and Potato Cakes

2 cups cooked meat, ground
2 cups mashed potatoes
2 eggs
1 small onion, minced fine
½ cup tomato juice
1 teaspoon salt
   pepper to taste

Combine meat, mashed potatoes, eggs, onion, tomato juice and seasonings. Shape into 8 patties in greased baking dish and brush with melted butter. Bake in oven, 350 degrees, for 30 minutes.

— *Ike Hawkins, Clifton, Arizona*

Tamale Pie

1 cup yellow cornmeal
2 cups milk
3 eggs, beaten
1 can tomatoes
1 can yellow whole-kernel corn
1 pound lean ground beef
2 onions, chopped
½ cup oil
1 tablespoon salt
3 chili peppers
1 teaspoon pepper
2 cups ripe olives, pitted

Combine cornmeal with milk and eggs in a saucepan. Cook until thick, add tomatoes and corn. Let simmer while preparing meat. Brown onions and meat in hot oil; stir in seasonings, add to cornmeal mixture. Stir in olives. Pour all into a large greased baking dish. Bake in moderate oven, 375 degrees, for 1 to 1½ hours. Or bake in dutch oven with moderate coals about same length of time. Serves 8.

— *Bill Smith, Boquillas Cattle Co. (Wagon Rod)*

Bernaise Sauce for Steak

Put 2 tablespoonfuls, each, of fine chopped green pepper and mild onion (shallot) and ¼ cup of vinegar to simmer on the back of the range. When the moisture has nearly evaporated, add 2 tablespoonfuls of butter and the beaten yokes of 3 eggs. Set the saucepan in a dish of boiling water. Stir and let cool, adding twice meanwhile, 2 more tablespoonfuls of butter. When the sauce thickens, season with salt and pepper and strain. The sauce may also be used without straining.

Cook steaks an inch and a half thick from eight to ten minutes. Set the steaks on a hot platter and spread with Bernaise sauce.

— *"Barney" Borneman, Eagle Creek, Arizona*

One Shot Pot

Early in the morning cut up stew meat in small pieces (beef or venison), onions, garlic, celery (celery salt will do fine). Cook until tender which will take about two hours. Then add a can of tomatoes, 1 can of corn, 1 can of green beans and 1 can peas.

If no canned goods available you can add one cup macaroni, 1 cup rice and several diced potatoes. This is called Slum-gullion in some parts of the West.

— *Bill Smith, Boquillas Cattle Co. (Wagon Rod)*

Tom Fuller

I don't know where this dish got its name but I got the recipe at "Bug Point" not far from Dove Creek, Colorado, back in the early forties.

Peel enough potatoes (1 large potato per person). 1 large onion added to potatoes, salt and pepper and enough water to stew potatoes until done. Meanwhile brown several slices of bacon in skillet (or small diced pieces of ham will do) add to potatoes, grease and all. Lastly add 1 can drained yellow whole kernel corn. Cream style may be used but makes stew too soupy. Even better is 2 cups of fresh corn cut from cob and cooked with potatoes.

— *Verena Beasley, Dove Creek, Colorado and St. Johns, Arizona*

Game Marinade

3 onions minced
1 cup diced carrots
1 cup chopped green onions
1 cup tarragon vinegar
5 cups dry white wine
1 clove garlic, crushed
2 teaspoons salt
1 teaspoon fresh ground pepper
2 bay leaves
1 cup diced celery

Combine all in saucepan and cook about five minutes. Cool. Pour over steaks or roast venison, elk, antelope or bear. Keep submerged and turn daily. Let meat marinate in cool place three or four days.

— *Alvin Clary, Globe, Arizona*

Venison Stew (sweet-sour)

2 or 3 pounds venison stew meat, cut into small chunks
2 or 3 tablespoons bacon drippings
1 large can solid pack tomatoes
1 onion, diced
1 clove garlic, minced, or 1 teaspoon garlic salt
⅓ cup brown sugar
½ cup wine vinegar

Brown stew meat in the fat. Add tomatoes, onion, garlic, brown sugar, and vinegar; and simmer 2 hours. Salt to taste. Carrots and potatoes may be added to stew if desired.

— *Dutch Charley, Double Circle Ranch, Eagle Creek, Arizona*

Bear Meat With Juniper Berries

Roast the saddle (the double loin) in deep dutch oven. Baste with 2 cups red table wine to which has been added 1 large diced onion and 2 teaspoons crushed juniper berries. If the bear meat is not fat, then roast must be larded with bacon slices or salt pork. Salt and pepper to taste.

Bear meat can be cooked in the same way as beef: steaks, roasts, pot roast, and bearburgers.

— *Alvin Clary, Globe, Arizona*

Venison, Elk, or Antelope

Trim the fat away — all of it — no matter how young the animal may be. Wash with vinegar and wipe dry. Pierce the roast and push strips of pork or fatty bacon (salt pork) into the cavities. Lay strips of bacon or pork on roast or tie on with string.

Salt and pepper and dust with flour. Preheat dutch oven and add beef suet. Sear roast on all sides. Add one large onion sliced, two cloves of garlic. Add one cup of hot water, one can of tomatoes or tomato sauce. Some wine and condiments may be added. Cover and simmer until done. Or this roast may be buried in fire pit. A large roast will require seven or eight inches of red coals and is best if wood has been burned in pit instead of using hot coals from the cooking fire. Put red coals on top of oven and then six inches of dry dirt tamped down. Be sure there are no air holes. It will take six or seven hours for a ten pound roast.

This is best method to roast game. Wild meat is not marbled like beef and takes slow simmering under cover to make tough game tender.

A can of mushrooms added to the juices makes a delicious gravy.

Dutch Oven Turkey

If bird is young, disjoint, dredge in flour, salt, and pepper. Brown all pieces in bacon fat in dutch oven. Add two cups of hot water, put on lid and place oven on bed of hot coals. Cover lid with coals and bank coals around oven. Cook about four hours. Small amounts of water can be added when needed. A bay leaf or sliced onion can be added if desired.

— Herb Nichols, Clifton, Arizona

Breads and Pancakes

Sourdough Starters

1. Take 4 cups water in which potatoes have been boiled. Add 4 cups flour, 2 teaspoons salt and 2 teaspoons sugar. Mix well and put in crock and cover. Let stand several days in warm place until fermentation begins.

2. In 2 cups water (warm) dissolve 1 cake yeast or 1 package of dry yeast. Mix 2 cups flour. Let stand in covered crock in warm place for twenty-four hours and batter will be ready to use.

3. Take 2½ cups flour, 2 teaspoons sugar and 2 teaspoons salt. Then take 1 cup milk and add 2 teaspoons vegetable oil and bring to boil. Cool and dissolve 1 package dry yeast. Blend in dry ingredients. Cover and let stand in warm place twenty-four hours.

Clair's Dry Yeast

Heat two quarts of buttermilk just to boiling point. Then add enough cornmeal to make a thick mush and boil about five minutes. Then put the mush in a crock and cool to lukewarm. Add three cakes of moist commercial yeast dissolved in a cup of warm water. Stir well and place the crock of mush in a warm place to stand overnight. The next morning add enough dry cornmeal to make a stiff dough, stiff enough to make small cakes shaped with the hands. Put the cakes in a porous sack and hang in a perfectly dry place. This recipe makes from fifty to sixty cakes and when using to make bread use one cake to a pint of liquid.

— *Clair Haight, Hashknife Outfit, Winslow, Arizona*

[119]

Sourdough Biscuits

½ cup starter
2½ cups flour
¾ teaspoon salt
½ teaspoon soda
1 cup milk
1 tablespoon sugar
1 teaspoon baking powder
   bacon grease

Mix starter, milk, and 1 cup of the flour in a large bowl the night before. Cover and keep in warm place.

Next morning turn sourdough out onto breadboard with 1 cup flour. Combine salt, sugar, baking powder and soda into remaining ½ cup flour and sift over top of dough. With hands, mix dry ingredients into soft dough, kneading lightly. Roll out 1 inch thick. Cut biscuits with cutter, dip in warm grease, and place close together in pan. Place in warm place to rise about ½ hour. Bake in moderate hot oven 375 to 400 for 30 minutes.

— *Clair Haight, Hashknife Outfit, Winslow, Arizona*

Sourdough Cornbread

    1 cup starter
       cornmeal, enough to make a beatable batter
 1½ cups milk
    2 tablespoons sugar
    2 eggs, beaten
  ¼ cup warm melted butter, or fat
  ½ teaspoon salt
  ½ teaspoon soda

Mix starter, cornmeal, milk, eggs and stir thoroughly in large bowl. Stir in melted butter, salt and soda. Turn into a 10-inch greased frying pan or dutch oven, and bake for 25 to 30 minutes.
— *Clair Haight, Hashknife Outfit, Winslow, Arizona*

Sourdough Pancakes

The evening before, put cup of sourdough starter in large bowl. (Do not use metal.) Add 2 cups lukewarm water and 2½ cups of flour. Mix well. Cover bowl and set in warm place.

In the morning put 1 cup starter back in sourdough pot. To your pancake batter add 1 egg, 2 tablespoons oil, ¼ cup milk, mix. Then blend 1 teaspoon salt, 1 teaspoon soda and 2 tablespoons sugar, and sprinkle over batter and fold gently. Do not beat. A slight foaming action will start. Let rest 5 minutes, then drop with tablespoon to make small pancakes on hot, lightly greased griddle. If batter is too thick add a small amount of milk. Sourdough pancakes require a somewhat hotter griddle.
— *Clair Haight, Hashknife Outfit, Winslow, Arizona*

Old Time Potato Bread

1 potato
   water
2 packages dry yeast
2 tablespoons melted shortening
2 tablespoons sugar
1 tablespoon salt
1 cup warm milk
6½ to 7½ cups unsifted all purpose flour

Pare and dice potato; boil in water to cover, until tender. Drain; reserving liquid to make 1 cup; cool. Mash potato and set aside.

Pour warm potato water into large bowl. Sprinkle in dry yeast; stir until dissolved. Add shortening, sugar and salt. Stir in mashed potato, warm milk and 3 cups flour; beat until smooth. Stir in enough additional flour to make a stiff dough. Turn out on lightly floured board and knead until smooth and elastic.

Place in greased bowl, turning to grease top. Cover; let rise in warm place until double in size, about thirty minutes.

Punch dough down; turn over in bowl. Cover and let rise again for about twenty minutes. Punch dough down and turn onto lightly floured board; divide in half. Shape into loaves and place in 2 greased loaf pans. Cover with cloth and let rise until doubled in bulk. Bake at 375 for about forty minutes, or until done. Remove from pans and cool on rack.

— *Verena Beasley, Dove Creek, Colorado, and St. Johns, Arizona*

Vinegar Biscuits

Take two quarts of flour, 1 large tablespoonful of lard or butter, 1 tablespoonful and a half of vinegar and stir it well; stir in flour, beat 2 eggs very light and add to it. Make a dough with warm water stiff enough to roll out, and cut with a biscuit cutter one inch thick and bake in a quick oven.

— *Alma Sloan, Clifton, Arizona*

Baking Powder Biscuits

3 cups flour
6 teaspoons baking powder
3 tablespoons fat (lard or bacon drippings)
Approx. 1 cup milk
1 teaspoon salt
1 tablespoon sugar

Sift together dry ingredients, then rub in lard with fingertips, until flaky. Pour about a cupful milk to moisten. Turn out on well floured board and pat about ½ inch thickness. Cut with biscuit cutter and place in greased dutch oven that has been slightly preheated. Biscuits should be touching but not crowded. Place preheated lid on oven and cover with hot coals. Place oven on bed of good red coals and let bake about twenty minutes or until brown on top and bottom.
— *Clair Haight, Hashknife Outfit, Winslow, Arizona, 1922*

Sour Milk Biscuits

To baking powder biscuits recipe add sour milk instead of fresh milk, and add 1 teaspoon soda and leave out 3 teaspoons baking powder.
— *Clair Haight, Hashknife Outfit, Winslow, Arizona, 1922*

Sally Lunn

This is a batter bread.
Take 3½ to 4 cups unsifted all purpose flour, divided
⅓ cup sugar
 1 teaspoon salt
 1 package dry yeast
½ cup milk
½ cup water
½ cup softened shortening or butter
 3 eggs

Thoroughly mix 1¼ cups flour, the sugar, salt and undissolved yeast in a large bowl. Combine milk, water and shortening in a saucepan. Heat over low heat until liquids are warm. Gradually add to dry ingredients and beat 2 minutes. Add eggs and 1 cup flour, or enough flour to make a thick batter. Beat 2 more minutes. Stir in enough additional flour to make a stiff batter. Cover; let rise in warm place until doubled in bulk. About 1 hour. Then stir batter down and beat as well as you can, about ½ minute. Turn into a well-greased 9-inch pan. Cover and let rise about 1 hour. Bake at 325 about 45 or 50 minutes or until done. This is best served warm. It should be broken apart with a fork, never cut with a knife.

— *Verena Beasley, Dove Creek, Colorado and St. Johns, Arizona*

Slappers

Put 2 cups cornmeal in a bowl with ½ teaspoon salt and 2 tablespoons of butter. Pour on slowly sufficient boiling water to thoroughly moisten without being sloppy, cover, and let stand overnight.

In the morning, add 3 well beaten eggs, 1 cup milk and 1 cup flour mixed with 2½ teaspoons baking powder. This makes a very thick batter. Drop by spoonfuls on a hot greased griddle, cook slowly until brown. Butter each slapper as it is taken from the griddle and serve with pork sausage or chops.

— *Blackie Clingman, Globe, Arizona*

Humpy's Fried Cornmeal Bread

4 or 5 good handfuls of yellow cornmeal
Hunk of lard size of an egg
2 pinches salt
3 large pinches sugar

Mix all together and pour over enough boiling water to make a batter. Fry as hot cakes. Good with beans or turnip greens.
— *Humpy, Cook for Hashknife Outfit, Winslow, Arizona*

Rice Pancakes

1 cup flour
1½ gills cooked rice (¾ cup)
3 teaspoonfuls baking powder
1 egg well beaten
1 teaspoonful salt
2 teaspoonfuls sugar
1 gill milk (½ cup)
1 tablespoonful melted butter or lard

Mix and sift flour, salt and sugar. Add rice and melted butter, the egg and milk. Beat. Cook at once on hot well greased griddle. Serve hot with butter and syrup.
— *Clair Haight, Hashknife Outfit, Winslow, Arizona*

Virginia Corn Cakes

2 eggs
1½ gills milk (¾ cup)
½ tablespoonful sugar
1½ gills canned corn (¾ cup)
1 level tablespoonful baking powder
1 cup flour
½ teaspoonful salt

Beat eggs, add milk and sugar, stir in canned corn. Sift flour, baking powder, and salt together and stir into the corn mixture and bake in muffin tins or can be baked in dutch oven. Cook hot and fast at 450 degrees. This makes only enough for a few. Double or triple recipe when cooking for a bunch of cowhands.
— *Clair Haight, Hashknife Outfit, Winslow, Arizona*

Beans, Potatoes and Rice

Sheepherder's Scalloped Potatoes

Home from the hill — the hunter finds a ready-to-eat gourmet dinner if he has had the forethought to prepare a dutch oven meal early that morning.

Necessary are a dozen pork chops (or thick slices of ham or lamb chops) and a 14- or 16-inch dutch oven.

Melt a little fat in the bottom of the oven and place meat in oven and brown lightly on both sides. Remove and place to one side.

Slice enough raw potatoes to half fill the oven. Slice two large onions and mix with potatoes. Leave the pork grease in bottom of oven and put in layers of potatoes and onions with salt, pepper and flour. Place all the pork chops on top and cover with milk (canned or powdered milk).

Dig hole large enough to hold about six inches of good hardwood coals. Place oven in hole and cover with hot coals. Foil or a small piece of tin placed on top of oven before adding coals will aid in removing later when done. Cover all with at least six inches of dirt.

Meat and potatoes will be done in four hours but can be left in hole for eight or ten hours if necessary. Do not remove until ready to eat.

How To Prepare Fire Hole

Dig hole in good well-drained area not too close to large trees (the roots hinder diggin'). For one-pot meals, beans or roasts, the hole should be at least two feet deep by two and a half feet wide at the top. Burn hardwood in the hole for at least an hour. There must be six inches of good red coals for meat dishes and more for bean-hole beans. Be sure hole is not wet. If hole is damp you may have to burn fire longer period of time.

Be sure no large burning chunks or pieces of charred wood are in the hole when oven is put in. Just good red coals with some blue flame.

Bean-hole Beans

   2 cups pinto beans
  ½ pound salt pork
   1 medium onion
   1 clove garlic
1½ quarts water

Wash beans and put into 8 pound lard bucket with water, salt pork, onions, and garlic. If pork is very salty you need not salt beans. Add pepper to taste. Put lid on tight and bury pail in bed of coals and cover completely with dirt. Leave overnight.

Be sure there are no airholes for heat to escape. At least a foot of dirt packed smoothly is best.

Spanish Rice #1

   6 slices bacon, cut up
   1 small onion, finely chopped
  ½ bell pepper, chopped (optional)
   3 cups cooked rice
   2 cups canned tomatoes
Salt and pepper to taste
Powdered chili, if desired

Fry bacon until crisp, drain off most of fat, add onion, bell pepper and rice and tomatoes. Cook over low heat about 15 minutes. Or bake in slow dutch oven until done.

— *Ermajean Wayt, Longmont, Colorado*

Spanish Rice #2

Put two frying pans on the stove, and in each put one teaspoonful of bacon fat. Take one onion and four green chilies, chop very fine, sprinkle with a little salt; put this in one frying pan and cook until softened without browning. In the other pan put in one cup rice, washed and dried; stir and let cook a light brown; add the onion and chilies and one cup of canned tomatoes; then fill the frying pan with boiling water and let cook until rice is dry. Black pepper may be added to taste.

This is a good dutch oven dish also.

Sweet Potato Cakes

6 medium sized sweet potatoes, 2 well beaten eggs, 1 tablespoon butter, 2 tablespoons sugar, add pepper and salt to taste.

Boil potatoes. When tender, mash very fine, add beaten eggs and seasoning. Add flour to make a stiff dough, roll out, cut with biscuit cutter, dip in beaten eggs, then crumbs, and fry in deep fat.

Mashed Potato Patties

Use leftover mashed potatoes that are well seasoned with milk and butter. To each 2 cups of mashed potatoes add one well beaten egg and 1 heaping tablespoon flour. Mix well and drop by tablespoonfuls on hot griddle. When brown turn once and brown on the other side.

A nice variation is to add some well-drained yellow corn. Or a small amount of shredded sharp cheese.

Cakes, Cookies and Doughnuts

Clair's Pork Cake

One teacupful of chopped pork, salt and fat
One cup of sugar, lightest brown for that;
One teacup of molasses, and one cup
Of boiling water on the pork poured up;
One teacup raisins seeded and chopped fine,
One teacup currants, heaping, I opine.
One teacup citron and of brandy, two
Tablespoonfuls; one nutmeg; flour stirred through.
One teaspoonful soda, and one each,
Of every spice you have within your reach.
Teaspoonful salt, but with the pork, not flour.
Bake in a slow oven for an hour.

Use enough flour so that batter will pour sluggishly into baking pan.

— *Clair Haight, Hashknife Outfit, Winslow, Arizona*

Eggless Cake

2 cups brown sugar
2 cups boiling water
4 tablespoons melted lard (or butter if you have it)
1 teaspoon salt
1 teaspoon cinnamon
1 teaspoon allspice
1 tablespoon cocoa (or chocolate)
1 cup raisins

Boil all ingredients 4 or 5 minutes, let cool, then add 3 cups flour, 2 teaspoons soda, sifted with the flour. Bake 1 hour in a slow oven in loaf pan.

— *Clair Haight, Hashknife Outfit, Winslow, Arizona*

Eggless Chocolate Cake

Melt three tablespoonfuls lard or butter. When cooled some add 1 cupful sugar and six teaspoonfuls cocoa. Sift 1½ cups flour with 1 teaspoonful soda and one teaspoonful salt. Stir into cocoa, mix alternately with 1 cupful buttermilk. Sprinkle nuts on top if you have them. Grease and flour pan and bake in moderate oven about 35 minutes. Very good.

— *Alma Sloan, Clifton, Arizona*

Potato Cake

2 cups of sugar creamed with 1 cup of lard, butter if you have it. Then add 1 cup finely mashed potatoes, yokes of 4 eggs, beaten until light, and ½ cup sweet milk. Now sift 2 cups flour, 1 cup ground or grated chocolate, 2½ teaspoons baking powder, 1 teaspoon cinnamon, ½ teaspoon cloves, ½ teaspoon allspice, ½ teaspoon salt.

Commence adding the flour mixture, beating well between times, and add a cup of chopped nuts and a cup of seeded raisins, if you wish. Lastly fold in the stiffly whisked whites of the eggs. Bake in a moderately slow oven and watch it carefully that it does not burn.

— *Alma Sloan, Clifton, Arizona*

Poorman's Cake
(no eggs or milk)

Put 1 cup raisins in saucepan with 2 cups water. Cook about 15 minutes. While still warm add 1 cup shortening, 1 cup white sugar and 1 cup brown sugar. Let cool. Then add 4 cups flour, 1 teaspoon baking powder, ½ teaspoon soda and 1 teaspoon each of allspice, cloves, nutmeg, and cinnamon with ½ teaspoon salt. Put in greased and floured pan and cook in slow oven at least 45 minutes or until done.

Variations: you can substitute molasses for brown sugar. You can add any cooked fruit you may have on hand — such as applesauce or any cooked dried fruit. Be sure it is drained well before adding to batter.

You can add a cup of chopped nuts and 1 cup of diced pineapple, but if you have nuts and pineapple you're not a poorman.

Cooked prunes can be added instead of raisins. Using prunes doesn't disqualify you as a poorman.

— *Iva Simon, Limon, Colorado*

Sourdough Chocolate Cake

    1 cup starter
    1 cup milk
    1 cup sugar
    ½ cup shortening
    ½ teaspoon salt
 1½ teaspoons baking soda
    1 teaspoon vanilla
    1 teaspoon cinnamon
    2 eggs
    3 squares semi-sweet chocolate melted
    2 cups flour

Prepare a cup of thick sourdough starter the night before. Let rise in warm spot.

Cream sugar and shortening together. Add eggs. Add sourdough starter, milk, vanilla, cinnamon, and melted chocolate. Beat at least 2 minutes. Into flour blend salt and soda, and add to mixture, fold in gently but thoroughly. Pour into greased and floured cake pans. Bake at 350 degrees for 35 to 40 minutes.

— *Clair Haight, Hashknife Outfit, Winslow, Arizona*

Aunt Ann Pudding

Make a plain cake using eggs if you have them. When cake is done, turn out on board and when cool, split in half. Spread the bottom half with well spiced applesauce made from dried apples (not too soupy). Cover with the top half and spread the top with lemon sauce made with or without eggs.

— Blackie Clingman, Globe, Arizona

Jelly Cake

Make a plain cake in dutch oven and when cool take out and split in half. Spread jam or jelly or whatever you have in the way of sweets. Cover with top half. Sprinkle with powdered sugar or drizzle with melted brown sugar and butter.

— Blackie Clingman, Globe, Arizona

Mincemeat Cookies

 ¾ cup shortening
1½ cups sugar
 3 eggs
 1 cup mincemeat
 3 cups flour
 1 teaspoon soda
   salt
 1 cup broken nut meats

Cream shortening and sugar; add eggs, beating well; add mincemeat. Sift dry ingredients and stir in. Add nuts. Drop by spoonfuls onto greased cookie sheet. Bake 350 degrees about 15 minutes. Makes a bunch.

— Alma Sloan, Clifton, Arizona

Spice Sourdough Cake

Use spices, walnuts and raisins in sourdough chocolate cake recipe and omit chocolate.

— Clair Haight, Hashknife Outfit, Winslow, Arizona

Dutch Oven Doughnuts

1 egg and 1 yolk
1 cup sugar
2 cups milk
½ teaspoon salt
4 teaspoons baking powder
¼ teaspoon nutmeg
4 or 5 cups flour

Beat egg well and add sugar and milk. Sift salt, baking powder, nutmeg, and flour together and add to mixture. Roll to ½ inch thickness. Cut with doughnut cutter and fry in deep hot fat. Drain on unglazed paper.

Points on Frying Doughnuts

To prevent large cracks when frying, have the dough soft. Turn the cakes as they come to the top of the fat and often during the cooking. Too much flour makes dry, hard doughnuts.

An extra yolk of egg will furnish fat enough to do away with addition of butter or other form of fat.

Use fat that has not been previously used for frying. Vegetable fats burn less readily than animal fats and also give a better texture and flavor to the foods cooked in them.

Frying fat which is no longer in good condition for cooking foods may be strained and used in soap making.

— *Clair Haight, Hashknife Outfit, Winslow, Arizona*

Potato Doughnuts

2 medium potatoes
2 tablespoonfuls of lard or good clean drippings
2 well beaten eggs
1½ cups sugar
1 gill milk (½ cup)
3 teaspoonfuls baking powder
5 cups flour

Boil and mash potatoes, stir in butter or lard while potatoes are still hot. Then add eggs, sugar, milk and flour sifted with the baking powder. Knead on floured board. Cut and fry in deep fat. Makes about fifty doughnuts.

— *Clair Haight, Hashknife Outfit, Winslow, Arizona*

Pies

Bear Fat Pie Crust

Pass together through a sieve three cups of sifted pastry flour, half a teaspoonful of salt, and half a teaspoonful of baking powder. With a knife or the tips of the fingers work into this mixture from ⅔ to ¾ cup of bear fat. When fat is well mixed, add gradually, mixing meanwhile, with a knife, enough cold water to make a paste that sticks together. Turn on a board lightly dredged with flour and roll with a rolling pin. This will make two pies.

— *Clair Haight, Hashknife Outfit, Winslow, Arizona*

Vinegar Cobbler

    4 cups sugar
2½ cups water
    ¾ cup vinegar
    ¼ pound butter
        nutmeg to suit

Put all ingredients in pan you are going to bake in, or use dutch oven. Let mixture boil while you make pie dough. Roll out pie dough thin and cut into strips. Crisscross on top of hot vinegar solution. Bake in medium oven until crust is brown.

Sourdough dumplings can be used instead of pie dough. If pie is thin, that's the way it should be. This is not a custard pie, and best baked in dutch oven in camp. If you don't think it is good just try it!

— *Bessie Filleman, 4 Bar Ranch, Eagle Creek, Arizona*

Mock Pecan Pie (pinto bean)

1 cup mashed pinto beans
2 cups sugar
4 eggs
¼ pound butter (or margarine)
2 tablespoons molasses or dark corn syrup
2 teaspoons vanilla
½ teaspoon salt

Cream sugar and butter. Add well-beaten eggs, molasses, and salt. Beat in well-mashed beans. Beans must have been cooked un-seasoned and well done. Pour into unbaked pie shell and bake at 350° until firm. Pecans or chopped walnuts may be sprinkled on top before baking.

It's fun to fool your family and friends. They will never guess this delicious pie is made from the lowly frijole.

— *Lois Bowman, Wickenburg, Arizona*

Raisin Pie

Line a pie tin with rich pastry, fill with a cup and a half of seeded raisins, ¾ of a cup of sugar mixed with 2 tablespoonfuls of flour, the juice of 1 lemon, ½ cup of water, ½ teaspoonful salt and a tablespoonful of butter in bits. Cover with pastry. Bake about 40 minutes.

Mock Mince Pie, Spring Style

Chop together 1 cup each of rhubarb and raisins. Add grated rind and juice of 1 lemon, 2 tablespoonfuls of butter, 1 cup of sugar, 1 egg well beaten, and mix thoroughly. Turn into a tin lined with pastry and dredge on a little flour and ½ teaspoonful of salt. Bake with two crusts. Use spices if desired.

Sweet Potato Pie

Boil sweet potatoes until well done. Peel and slice them very thin. Line a deep pie pan with good plain pastry, and arrange the sliced potatoes in layers, dotting with butter and sprinkling sugar, cinnamon, and nutmeg over each layer, using at least ½ cup sugar. Pour over 3 tablespoonfuls whiskey, about ½ cup water, cover with pastry and bake. Serve warm.

Mock Cherry Pie

Cover the bottom of a pie plate with crust. Reserve enough for upper crust. For filling use 1 cup of cranberries, cut in halves; ½ cup of raisins, seeded and cut in pieces; ¾ cup of sugar; 1 tablespoon of flour; lump of butter, size of walnut. Bake 30 minutes in moderate oven. Some like a little more sugar.

— Blackie Clingman, Globe, Arizona

Molasses Pie

3   eggs
1   teacupful of brown sugar
½   of a nutmeg
2   tablespoonfuls of butter

Beat well together, stir in 1 teacupful of molasses with above ingredients. Bake in pastry shell. The juice of 1 lemon will improve it very much. Syrup may be used instead of molasses. This pie is a great favorite with children.

— Clair Haight, Hashknife Outfit, Winslow, Arizona

Pumpkin Pie (with eggs)

Choose a ripe, clear-skinned pumpkin. Cut it, take out the seeds and peel it, cutting it into small pieces. Put very little water with it, only enough to keep it from burning. When soft enough to mash through a colander, reduce it all in this manner: For every coffee cupful of pumpkin allow 4 eggs, 1 pint of milk, ¾ tablespoon ginger, 2 tablespoonfuls flour, 1 gill of molasses and ½ pound of brown sugar. Flavoring may be cinnamon instead of ginger if preferred. With pumpkin pie, the crust should be pricked and baked 3 minutes before the pumpkin mixture is poured in. Bake until done in medium hot oven.

— Clair Haight, Hashknife Outfit, Winslow, Arizona

Vinegar Pie

For 1 pie, take ½ cup of sugar
3 eggs, saving whites for top meringue
1 tablespoon butter
2 tablespoons vinegar
1 cup water
2 tablespoons flour

Season with nutmeg. Bake crust about half done before putting in filling. Bake in slow oven until custard is done.

Dried Apple Pie

Take 2 cups cooked dried apples, sugar to sweeten, spices, dash salt and sprinkle bits of butter over all. Put in lined pie tin, cover with crust and bake in moderate oven. When making dutch oven cobbler put cooked fruit in dutch oven, sweeten, spices, dash salt, and butter. Cover with dough, punch holes to let out steam and cook with slow coals under oven and hot coals on lid until crust is done. This pie is good with some raisins added when cooking the apples. Serve with a slab of good cheese if you have it. I always like to add a little lemon or vinegar to my cooked, dried apples. It gives pie a tart taste.

— Clair Haight, Hashknife Outfit, Winslow, Arizona

Pie Plant Pie (Rhubarb Pie)

3 cups pie plant (rhubarb)
1 tablespoonful flour
1 cup sugar
1 teaspoonful butter
   Pie crust for top and bottom

Wash pie plant, do not skin; cut in small pieces. Mix sugar and flour well with pie plant. Place in crust, dot with butter and cover with upper crust.

— Allen Hardt, Double Circle Ranch, Eagle Creek, Arizona

Puddings

Tallow Pudding

Cook in a pot several kinds of dried fruit; apples, peaches, apricots, and raisins. Chop up fine small pieces of good white tallow and add to fruit. Cook until done, not too soupy. Add sugar and spices. Cover with regular pie dough and bake in dutch oven until crust is light brown. This is a real dutch oven tallow pudding. Some think a tallow pudding has to be boiled in a sack.

— *Joe Filleman, Eagle Creek, Arizona*

Suet (Tallow) Pudding

2   cups raisins
1   cup chopped walnuts (black walnuts are fine)
1   cup dark brown sugar, firmly packed
1   cup chopped suet
2   teaspoons baking powder
1   teaspoon cinnamon
1   teaspoon nutmeg
1   teaspoon allspice
1   teaspoon salt
2   cups flour
1½ cups milk
1   cup chopped dried fruit (any kind, prunes, figs, apricots, etc.)

Chop into very small pieces 1 cup of suet, no pieces being larger than a bean. Combine with raisins, nuts, brown sugar, and chopped dried fruit. Then mix flour and spices and salt with baking powder. Add gradually to fruit mixture with milk, beating well. Put in flour sack or tie in large square of cloth. Put in kettle of boiling water and boil 3 hours, always keeping enough boiling water to cover pudding. When done, remove pudding from boiling water, and put on cloth to drain. After about ½ hour, untie cloth and turn pudding onto dish. Let chill. Slice and serve with hard sauce. This pudding will keep well and is similar to plum pudding.

This can be made in camp with molasses instead of brown sugar. Or can be made with white sugar instead of either brown sugar or molasses. This was a great favorite with chuck wagon cooks, being called a "Boy in a Bag" or "Bastard in a Bag."

Slim Ellison's Taller Puddin'

I call this "Taller Puddin'," and I perfer gut fat for the suet. Chop it up about like beans. Mix up your sweet dough, not too stiff. Put in a lot of razens and some salt and some sugar and cinnamon.

Stir in taller and scatter it around. Dump it in a salt sack and tie the top. Dump it in a pot of boilin' water and boil hell out of it till U think the taller is done, and the dough. Better to cook razens first and use a little of the juice. We called it "A boy in a sack" and the damned fools et it and called it good. Then make a white sauce, with cornstarch and vanilla flavor. This sauce was known as "Heifers' dee-light."   — *Slim Ellison, Globe, Arizona*

Coyote-ite
(Slim Ellison's Pudding)

When I was cookin' for Joe Bassett, I made a puddin' with white sauce, colored and flavored with scorched sugar. Dumped in fruit cocktail. Heavily spiced with allspice and cinnamon. Cowboys said it was good. They had to!

— *Slim Ellison, Globe, Arizona*

Indian Pudding

  3 cups cornmeal mush
  2 tablespoons flour
  5 beaten eggs
  ½ cup melted butter
  1 cup molasses
  ½ cup milk
     juice and rind of 1 lemon

Stir altogether and bake ½ hour in very moderate oven. This makes a damned good pudding! Serve with a sweet sauce.

— *Blackie Clingman, Globe, Arizona*

Rhubarb Pudding

Line your pudding dish with slices of bread and butter. Cover with cup of rhubarb, stewed with sugar, then slices of bread and butter, and so on alternately until your dish is full, having the rhubarb and sugar on top. Cover with plate and bake half an hour. This pudding is excellent with evaporated apricots or peaches instead of rhubarb.

Honey Pudding

To make this pudding, the hens must be laying more eggs than you can use, whenever that is.

Beat ½ pound honey with 6 ounces butter to a cream, and stir in 1 cup bread crumbs. Beat the yokes of 8 eggs, then add to the honey mixture; and beat Hell out of it for about 10 minutes or until your arm gives out. This pudding has to boil or steam, so put mix in a kettle or can; and put in pail of water (need not cover top), and steam for 1½ hours.

If making in camp, better put mix in a lard can, with a few holes punched in lid. Don't let boiling water get into pudding.

— *Blackie Clingman, Globe, Arizona*

Hominy Pudding

    1 cup boiled hominy
 1½ pints milk
    3 eggs
    1 tablespoon butter
    1 cup sugar

Pour into greased dutch oven, and bake about 20 minutes to ½ hour. Slow coals.

— *Clair Haight, Hashknife Outfit, Winslow, Arizona*

Green Corn Pudding

Take 24 full ears of sweet green corn. Score the kernels and cut them from the cob. Scrape off what remains on the cob with a knife. Add a pint and a half of milk. Add 4 eggs well beaten, ½ teacup flour, ½ teacup butter, a tablespoonful sugar, and salt to taste. Bake in a well-greased earthen dish about 2 hours. Put on table browned and smoking hot. Eat with plenty of fresh butter. This can be used as a dessert by serving a sweet sauce with it. When served plain with butter in answers as a side vegetable.

— *Alma Sloan, Clifton, Arizona*

Spotted Pup
(Rice Pudding)

Take whatever amount needed for hungry cowboys of nice fluffy, cooked rice. Put in dutch oven and cover with milk and well-beaten eggs. Add sugar to sweeten well, a dash of salt; raisins and a little nutmeg. Or vanilla can be used as flavoring. Bake in slow oven until egg mixture is done and raisins soft.

— *Clair Haight, Hashknife Outfit, Winslow, Arizona*

Plain Pup
(Same as *Spotted Pup* but omit the raisins)

When cooking in dutch oven be sure coals are not too hot as this pudding is best if it never boils. If it boils, eggs and milk curdle.

— *Clair Haight, Hashknife Outfit, Winslow, Arizona*

Bread Pudding

Break up any old leftover biscuits or sourdough bread. Mix soft with milk and sugar; some spices. Dump in some raisins and cook slow in dutch oven. If you have eggs you can add some to this pudding.   — *Slim Ellison, Globe, Arizona*

Humpy's Apple Dumplings

Use 1 quart flour. Sift through flour 1 teaspoon soda and 2 small spoonfuls cream of tartar. Mix in 1 tablespoon lard, 1 tablespoon cow butter if you have it, dissolved in small amount of hot water. Add enough milk to make a good dough. Roll the dough out to ¼ inch thick cut into squares big enough to contain ½ cup cooked apples. Bring corners of dough together and crimp edges to hold in juices. Drop in hot fat and fry until dough is brown, turning only once. Drain on brown paper bag. Serve hot. Be sure apples are not too soupy. Drain cooked apples well before putting in square of dough. These can be cooked in camp in dutch oven and other kinds of fruit can be used such as peaches, apricots and even prunes. Served with sugar and thick cream, they are a real delight.

Humpy, Cook for Hashknife Outfit, Winslow, Arizona

Mincemeat, Preserves, Wine and Soap

Cattle Drovers' Mincemeat

3 or 4 pounds venison well cooked
1 pound dried apples well cooked
2 pounds raisins
2 cups molasses
2 pounds brown sugar
1 teaspoonful each of all spices available such as cinnamon,
        nutmeg, and cloves
2 or 3 cups red wine or cider
1 teaspoonful salt

Grind cooked venison if you have a food chopper, if not, dice cooked meat very fine. Drain cooked dried apples and add to chopped meat. Grind raisins or chop mighty fine, add to meat and apples. Add spices, sugar, molasses, and salt along with 2 or 3 cups good red wine. If wine not available add cider. If neither wine nor cider available add 1 cup vinegar. Cook in large pot, stirring constantly until raisins are done. Do not scorch.

This is an old recipe and you can see most ranchers in the early days would have these ingredients. This mincemeat was used in pies or added to a sweet batter and cooked like cookies. We had to make do with what we had, and no fancy stuff added such as citrus or white sugar.

— *Clair Haight, Hashknife Outfit, Winslow, Arizona*

Venison Mincemeat

  4 pounds venison, cooked
  1 pound suet, cooked and chopped
  6 pounds apples, chop but do not peel
  1 quart apple juice
5½ pounds sugar
  2 pounds seedless raisins, chopped
  2 pounds light currants, chopped
 ½ cup candied citron
  1 cup candied orange peel
 ½ cup candied lemon peel
 ¼ cup candied ginger
  1 tablespoon cinnamon, 1 of allspice, 1 of cloves and
         1 of mace
  1 pint apple brandy
  1 pint sherry

Grind meat and suet through fine blade of meat grinder. Mix all except brandy and sherry. Bring to slow boil, simmer until mixture thickens. Add sherry and brandy and pour into crock. Can be sealed in hot sterilized jars or stored in crock in a cool place for weeks.

— Blackie Clingman, Globe, Arizona

Ranchers' Mincemeat

½ teaspoon each of cloves, allspice, cinnamon, and nutmeg
2 calves tongues, boiled until well done
2 pounds sugar
1 pound raisins
1 pound currants
¼ pound citron
3 pounds chopped apples
1½ pounds suet
1 tablespoon salt
    rind and juice of two oranges
    rind and juice of two lemons
¼ pound candied orange peel cut fine
¼ pound candied lemon peel cut fine
1 pint brandy
1 quart good whiskey

Peel and trim 2 calves tongues, cooked well done, put through grinder. Add sugar, raisins, currants, and citron. Mix well. Chop apples fine and add to meat. Add spices and suet and salt. Mix well. Pour over this the fruit juices, rind and peel, brandy and whiskey. Mix well. Put into a crock and cover with cloth and put on lid. Place in cool room for four weeks. When making pies if mixture is too thick moisten with a little brandy.

Apple Butter

10 pounds stewed apples (weigh apples raw)
 1 pint vinegar
 3 pounds sugar
    Boil about 1½ hours. Do not scorch.

— *Alma Sloan, Clifton, Arizona*

Prickly Pear Jelly

6½ cups prickly pear juice
½ cup lemon juice
9 cups sugar
2 packages Sure Jell

Do not peel prickly pears. Wear gloves and rub spines off with a gunny sack. Wash them well; it's not necessary for all spines to be removed. It's amazing how they disappear when cooked.

Put fully ripe fruit in kettle with a small amount of water. Not more than three cups for an eight quart kettle. Bring fruit to a boil, and mash with potato masher. Do not overcook. If pears are fully ripe, they will be fairly juicy. Drain through cloth.

Measure juice into large kettle and bring to boil. Add 2 packages of Sure Jell. Boil hard 1 minute. A full rolling boil that cannot be stirred down. Add lemon juice and sugar. Bring to hard boil, and let boil 1 full minute.

Be sure you measure exactly. If a more firm jelly is desired, omit ¼ cup of juice and add ½ cup sugar. Jelly will be a beautiful claret red and firm.

Prune Butter

2 pounds prunes, water
2 cups sugar
1 cup white or cider vinegar
1 teaspoon cinnamon and 1 of allspice
½ teaspoon nutmeg and ½ teaspoon cloves

Wash prunes, cover with water, and simmer for one hour. Cool and drain, remove pits. Mash, add remaining ingredients, and boil ten minutes. Put in hot sterilized jars and seal.

Dried Fruit Chutney

½ pound dried apples
½ pound dried peaches
½ pound dried apricots
½ pound dried dates
½ pound dried raisins
 2 cloves garlic, chopped fine
 1 pound sugar
 1 tablespoon allspice
 1 tablespoon salt
    Pinch cayenne pepper
1½ pints vinegar

Soak apples, peaches, and apricots in water overnight. Drain, cut into small pieces, stew until soft in part of the water drained off. Put dates and raisins through food chopper or grinder; add garlic and remaining ingredients to fruit. Cook 30 minutes or until chutney is thick and soft, stirring frequently. Pour into jars.

— *Verena Beasley, Dove Creek, Colorado, and St. Johns, Arizona*

Green Tomato Pickles

½ bushel green tomatoes
 6 large onions
 6 large peppers
¼ pound white mustard seed
 2 tablespoons celery seed

Chop altogether fine, put in layers, one of tomatoes and onions and one of salt, using in all ½ cup of salt. Let stand overnight.

In the morning, drain dry, and put on to boil in 2 quarts of vinegar. Cook until tender. When nearly done, add 1 pound of sugar. Put in jars while hot and seal.

— *Bessie Filleman, Eagle Creek, Arizona*

Peach Pickles

8 pounds of peaches
4 pounds of sugar
1 pint of vinegar
    Peel peaches. Stick 2 or 3 cloves in each whole peach. Add a few sticks of cinnamon. Cook 'til tender. Put in jars and seal, covering fruit fully with syrup. Use less sugar if desired.

Pickled Cabbage

2 heads cabbage (nice firm ones)
   salt
2 green peppers
2 cups sugar
2 cups cider vinegar
8 cups water
1 bay leaf
1 stick cinnamon
    Shred cabbage fine and let stand overnight in brine made of 1 part salt to 9 parts water. Drain water from cabbage in morning. Squeeze all water out. Chop green pepper and add to cabbage.
    Combine sugar, vinegar and water, add spices and bring to boil. Boil for 5 minutes. Pack cabbage in hot sterilized jars; pour boiling pickling liquid over cabbage. Seal at once and do not use for at least three weeks.
                        — *Bessie Filleman, Eagle Creek, Arizona*

Recipe for Preserving Eggs

    To each pailful of water add 2 pints of fresh slacked lime and 1 pint of common salt; mix well. Fill your barrel half full with fluid, put your eggs down in it at any time after June and they will keep two years if desired.
                        — *Clair Haight, Hashknife Outfit, Winslow, Arizona*

Spiced Watermelon Rind

9 cups (3 pounds) cubed white watermelon rind
   (remove dark green outer skin)
5 cups water
2 tablespoons salt
5 cups sugar
2 cups cider vinegar
1 tablespoon whole cloves
1 tablespoon whole allspice
1 tablespoon coarsely chopped stick cinnamon
1 lemon, sliced

Remove all green skin from rind (watermelons with thick rind make the best pickles). Cover melon rinds with 4 cups water. Add salt. Let stand overnight. Drain. Cover with more cold water in saucepan. Cook, covered over low heat until tender — about 2 hours. Drain.

Meanwhile, combine sugar, vinegar and remaining 1 cup cold water. Tie spices and lemon slices in cheesecloth bag. Drop into vinegar mixture. Boil 5 minutes. Then add watermelon rind and cook until rind is transparent — 45 to 60 minutes. Remove spice bag. Pack rind and syrup into jars and seal.

— Hazel House, Globe, Arizona

Dandelion Salad

Gather only freshly grown plants; best when the dew is on them. The tenderest leaves make an excellent salad with bacon dressing. The whole plant, after thorough washing, may be boiled until tender, drained, chopped fine, seasoned with salt, vinegar, and a liberal measure of butter. Those who think it too bitter may use half spinach, or beet, or sorrel, in which case the dandelion should be partly cooked before the more succulent plant is added. It cannot be too well recommended.

— Bessie Filleman, Eagle Creek, Arizona

Texas Butter

Texas butter is nothing but plain gravy made by adding flour to hot fat, browned, then adding water until thickened. If milk was available it was used instead of water. Salt and pepper to taste.

Charlie Taylor (a butter substitute)

Mix sorghum molasses and clean bacon fryings or other pure lard.

Estasmur (a spread for bread)

½ cup lard
¼ cup finely chopped onions
 1 tablespoon chopped parsley
     salt and pepper to taste
     Mix well. Serve on hot bread or toast.

Artificial Butter

Render beef suet at a very low temperature, churn in fresh buttermilk and yolks of eggs.

A Spread for Bread

Mix clean bacon drippings with a generous amount of fresh sweet cream. Add sugar and mix well. A drop of vanilla may be added.

Sun Dried Corn

Remove husks and silks from fully ripe corn. Drop corn in boiling, salted water, and cook until milk in the kernels sets, about 5 minutes. Remove corn from water. When cool enough to handle, cut corn off the cob. Spread kernels in a single layer in a shallow pan and cover lightly with a cloth. Place the pan in direct sunlight, taking indoors at night, until the kernels are thoroughly dry. This usually takes about two full days. Store at room temperature in covered jars.

When cooking, soak corn overnight or at least 4 hours. Boil until tender, drain, add butter, salt and pepper to taste. Or fry bacon in crisp bits and add small amount of red chili crumbled.

— *Clair Haight, Hashknife Outfit, Winslow, Arizona*

Dandelion Wine

2 quarts of dandelion blossoms
2 oranges, cut fine
2 lemons, skins and all
4 pounds of granulated sugar
4 quarts boiling water

Let stand 24 hours, strain and put in bottles or just let stand until thoroughly fermented. Bottle for use in November.

— *Hazel House, Globe, Arizona*

Fig Wine

8 pounds black figs
7 pounds sugar
1 yeast cake

Grind figs, then add sugar and 5 gallons water, and let set 14 days; and it will have the kick of ten mules!

— *Shorty Caraway, San Carlos, Arizona*

Ox-gall Soap

For washing woolens, silks, or fine prints liable to fade; 1 pint of beef gall, 2 pounds common bar soap cut fine, 1 quart boiling water (soft water); boil slowly, stirring occasionally until well mixed; pour into a vessel and when cold cut into pieces to dry.

A more simple way to use beef's gall, is to get a pint bottle filled with fresh beef's gall at the butchers, cork tightly and add to water when washing any material that is liable to fade; using more if articles are very liable to fade, and less if the liability is not so great. If gall gets stale, get some fresh.

Hard Soap

It is a simple matter to make hard soap, which is not only agreeable to use, but which has the great merit of cleanliness. To 7 pounds tallow use 3 pounds rosin, 2 pounds potash, and 6 gallons of water. Boil for three hours or longer. Turn from kettle into a washtub; let it stand all night. In the morning cut into bars and lay them on a table or board in the sun to harden for 2 or 3 days. This quantity will last a family of four persons a year if used for ordinary household purposes.

Washing Fluid

Dissolve in 1 gallon of hot water 1 pound concentrated lye, ½ ounce salts of tarter, ½ ounce liquid ammonia; when cool, bottle for use. Soak the clothes overnight; wring out and add 1 cup of fluid to boiler of water; put in clothes and boil for one hour; rub them as much as necessary. Then rinse well in 2 waters with a little bluing. This method will certainly save clothes, time, and labor.

A Good Way to Wash Clothes

Cut up a bar of soap (for an ordinary sized washing) in a dish and set on the stove; when melted put in 4 teaspoonfuls kerosene oil. Let this get good and hot and pour into a tub of water. Put your clothes in this and let them soak overnight. In the morning you will find that the clothes, with very few exceptions, will not need rubbing at all. Simply boil, rinse, and hang out. There, your washing is done, your back not broken, your knuckles not raw, and your clothes look as well as though you rubbed on them all day. Just try this once and you will rise up and bless us.

— From *Queen Of The Household*, 1882

Chili Sauce and Tomato Ketchup

Damned Hot Chili

1 gallon crushed ripe tomatoes (canned)
6 pounds green chilies, half red
3 pounds onions
15 to 18 large cloves fresh garlic
1½ quarts vinegar
1 pound sugar
1 tablespoon black pepper
2 tablespoons salt

Grind peppers, onions, and garlic in food chopper. Add vinegar, sugar, salt, and pepper. Add all to tomatoes and simmer at least one hour, stirring often. Can in hot sterilized jars at once. Makes at least 12 pints.

Barbecue Sauce

½ cup beef stock
½ cup vinegar
½ cup ketchup
  juice of 1 lemon
3 large onions, diced
½ cup brown sugar
⅔ cup water
1 tablespoon liquid smoke
2 teaspoons sugar
1½ teaspoons salt
½ teaspoon pepper
½ teaspoon cloves

Simmer for 1 hour or more. Serve on roast, ribs, or beefburgers.
— *Herb Nichols, Clifton, Arizona*

Arizona Tabasco Sauce

```
 3  dozen hot red peppers
1½  teaspoons horseradish
 1  cup cider vinegar
 1  clove garlic
 1  tablespoon sugar
 1  teaspoon salt
```

Cover peppers with water, add garlic, and cook until soft. Put peppers through a sieve. Add horseradish, sugar, salt, and vinegar. Simmer ten minutes. Pour into hot sterilized jars and seal at once.

— Blackie Clingman, Globe, Arizona

Red Hot Texas Sauce

```
24  long green peppers
12  ripe tomatoes
 4  cups vinegar
 1  cup sugar
 1  tablespoon salt
 2  tablespoons mixed spices
```

Remove seeds from peppers: *use rubber gloves to protect hands from being burned*. Chop peppers and tomatoes. Add 2 cups vinegar, boil until soft. Press through sieve, add sugar, salt, and spices in bag. Boil all until thick. Then add remaining 2 cups vinegar. Boil fifteen minutes more. Pour boiling hot into hot sterilized jars and seal at once.

— Blackie Clingman, Globe, Arizona

Tomato Sauce

To 2 gallons of strained tomatoes, add 1 dozen onions, 8 green peppers, chopped fine with the onions. Add, after the juice has been boiled down somewhat, 10 tablespoons brown sugar, the same of salt, 6 cupfuls white vinegar. Boil all together 1 hour. Bottle and seal.

— Bessie Filleman, Eagle Creek, Arizona

Tomato Ketchup

1   gallon strained tomatoes
4   tablespoons salt
3   tablespoons black pepper
3   tablespoons mustard
½   tablespoon cloves
½   tablespoon allspice
⅓   teaspoon red pepper
3   cloves garlic
1   pint vinegar

Boil until of the required thickness; put the dark spices and garlic into a cloth to prevent the ketchup from being dark.

— Bessie Filleman, Eagle Creek, Arizona

Home Remedies

The remedies that follow were discovered or improvised by frontier men and women who lived far from physicians, pharmacies, or even telephones. Some of the approaches seem bizarre — others obviously are based on common sense. All of them are folklore, to be read and enjoyed, but not to be confused with medical prescriptions or recommendation for actual use.

Grandmother's Salve for Everything

One pound rosin and ¼ cup mutton tallow after it is hard, half as much beeswax, and ¼ ounce camphor gum; put all into an old kettle, and let dissolve and just come to a boil, stirring with a stick; then take ¼ pail warm water, just the chill off, pour it in and stir carefully until you can get your hands around it; pull like candy until quite white and brittle; put a little grease on your hands to prevent sticking, and keep them wet. Wet the table, roll out the salve, and cut it with a knife. Keep it in a cool place.

Poultices

Bread and milk poultice: Put 1 tablespoon crumbs of stale bread into 1 gill of milk, let the whole boil once; or take stale bread crumbs, pour over them boiling water and boil until soft, stirring well; take from the fire and stir gradually in a little glycerine and sweet oil, so as to render the poultice pliable when applied. Use on any sore spot you can apply a poultice to — slivers, stitches, thorns, boils.

Mustard poultice to blister: Make a thick paste of mustard and water, spread it on a flannel, and cover its surface with fine muslin. A mustard plaster should remain on the patient only until skin becomes red, generally about 15 minutes.

Yeast poultice: for sores and indolent ulcers. Take 5 ounces yeast and 1 pound flour, or in that proportion, add water at blood heat, so as to form a tolerably stiff dough; set in warm place, but not so as to scald, until it begins to ferment or to "rise," and apply like any poultice.

A hop poultice: Boil 1 handful dried hops in ½ pint water until reduced to 1 gill, then stir in enough Indian meal to thicken it.

Tonics

A tea made from the bark of the dogwood tree is good for fever and ague. It is also used as an appetizer and tonic.

Wild cherry is used for general weakness, poor digestion, lack of appetite, nervousness and coughs. Mostly the parts of the inner bark of the roots and branches are dried and powdered. One heaping teaspoonful soaked in a quart of cold water for twenty-four hours makes a strong tea, and a wineglassful taken three or four times a day proves helpful.

Oak bark made into a strong tea is used for fever, ague, diarrhea, bleeding of the lungs. The acorns, when roasted, are regarded as a good remedy for scrofula and skin diseases. A poultice made of powdered bark will relieve pain, and is considered good for sores and ulcers.

The medicinal virtues of ginger tea in relieving colic, diarrhea, and indigestion are well known. A cupful of ginger tea, taken on going to bed, will break up a cold. Ginger tea is taken freely for any bowel trouble and is a good stimulant.

To Improve the Appetite

Dogwood, bruised, one ounce; water, one pint. Boil for fifteen minutes, strain, and add sufficient water through the strainer to make tea measure one pint. Mix. Dose: Wineglassful three times a day before meals.

Crust Coffee or Toast Water

Take stale crusts of bread, toast them nice dark brown — care to be taken they do not burn in the least, as that affects the flavor. Put the browned crusts into a large pitcher, and pour enough boiling water over to cover them; cover the pitcher closely, and let stand until cold. Strain and sweeten to taste. Reheat to boiling point when ready to serve or use as an iced drink.

Beef Tea

In the preparation of beef tea, according to the following recipe, the albumen of the tissue is preserved in a fluid form and is easily assimilated, forming a true food. Take 1 pound fresh beef off the round, and scorch quickly and very lightly on one side before the coals, cut it up fine as hash, put it in an earthen bowl and pour on ½ pint tepid water (not over 90 degrees F.) and let it stand for 2 hours in summer temperature near the stove, covered by a saucer, on the kitchen mantelpiece. Then strain and squeeze through clean linen, take the expressed juice and put it in a thick pie dish on the back of the stove, and stir steadily for 5 or 10 minutes. Never let it get warmer than 150 degrees F. Try the temperature by the finger. When it takes a darker hue, as butternut or walnut shade, it is done; season with a little salt. If you heat it up too hot all the albumen will coagulate, and it will be spoiled as a food. You may depend upon the deepening of the color. This beef juice has a cooked flavor and is of a port wine color. It is a valuable food.

A Cure for That Tired Rundown Feeling

How often we hear women who do their own work say that by
the time they have prepared a meal, and it is ready for the table they
are too tired to eat. One way to mitigate this evil is to take, about
half an hour before dinner, a raw egg, beat it until light, put in a
little sugar, flavor it, and drink it down. It will remove the faint,
tired-out feeling, and will not spoil your appetite for dinner. Plenty
of fresh air in the kitchen does a good deal to relieve this trouble,
and you do not take your dinner in "at the pores," as Dickens' old
Joey declared he took in the wine.

— From *Queen of the Household*

Rope Burns or Scalds

Cowboy urine has been used with great success for rope burns
or slight scalds.

Dysentery

Prickly pear cactus, split and roasted and the pulp eaten, is
very good for dysentery. The Southwestern Indians have used this
remedy for centuries.

Tea made from the Manzanita leaf or pink bark of the live oak
is good for relief of dysentery.

Sassafras is a very common remedy. The bark boiled into a tea
makes a pleasant drink, and will relieve dysentery and inflammation
of the bladder. When applied externally, it is found a good remedy
for relieving inflammation of the eyes.

Often the source of supply of the best remedies is readily at
hand. *The root of blackberry* is used for diarrhea, dysentery, and
"summer complaint" in children.

Wounds and Old Obstinate Sores

The Black Elder is used in the form of the flowers, the berries, and the bark. An ointment, made by stirring the fresh flowers into melted lard or vaseline, and subsequently strained, is good for burns, scalds, wounds, and old obstinate sores. The berries are laxative, and are good for rheumatism, gout, skin diseases, and habitual constipation. Often the berries are dried or canned as in preserving any other fruit.

Neuralgia

Macerate the leaves of the *common field thistle,* and use as a poultice on the parts affected, while a small quantity of the same is boiled down to the proportion of 1 quart to 1 pint, and a small wine-glassful of the concoction is drunk before each meal. A friend says he has never known it to fail of giving relief, while in almost every case it has effected a cure.

Snake Bite

Apply to the wound at once a freshly killed animal or chicken.
Mud packs applied to the wound should give some relief. Turpentine and gunpowder are good for snake bite. Kerosene and salt or tobacco juice are good snake bite remedies.

Delirium Tremens

A teaspoonful of red pepper, mixed with molasses, and taken in one dose is considered one of the best remedies for delirium tremens and seasickness.

Wind in the Stomach

Sage tea is an excellent recipe for flatulence, or wind in the stomach. It is also known to be good for colds or night sweats. A dose is a cupful of strong tea several times a day or as emergency demands.

Rheumatism

Cases of old or chronic rheumatism are often improved by sulphur baths and sulphur tea. It is also used as a cure for the itch and is good for loosening the bowels. A dose is a teaspoonful of powdered sulphur and molasses twice a day.

Ringworm

A very simple, yet effective cure for ringworm is to place on the affected part, for a short time every night, a copper coin which has remained for some time in vinegar, and is still wet with the liquid. It is also well to bathe the ringworm with a solution of 2 grains iodide of potash in 1 ounce water.

Another cure for ringworm is gunpowder applied three times a day. Or place a copper penny in butter until it turns green. Rub the green salve on the ringworm.

Ivy Poisoning

Rub wood ashes on the poisoned member. Ashes have proved a cure for ivy poisoning in all cases. Another cure for ivy poisoning is making a poultice from bruised leaves of the nightshade (*Solanum niger*) and cream. It is safe, sure, speedy, and effectual.

Nosebleed

Hold a nickel in the mouth. Or place a folded piece of paper or cardboard under the upper lip.

For nosebleed that cannot be stopped by other means, use the plant called Devil's Snuff (a fungus, so not really a plant, is it?). It comes on thin soils by the roadside and in the vicinity of decaying oak stumps, growing flat on the surface of the ground, sometimes in patches of a dozen in a small space about the size of a walnut. In the fall it begins to dry, and when dry, you may tread upon it and a profuse cloud of dark brown snuff is puffed up from the top of the fungus.

The powder should be snuffed up the nostrils and the bleeding will cease as soon as the contact is made. This powder is called "Devil's Snuff."

This powder can be gathered in the fall and stored in airtight containers. It must not be allowed to become damp in any way.

Headache

Headache will yield to the simultaneous application of hot water to the feet and back of neck.

Whooping Cough

Take 1 gill each of garlic, sweet oil and honey, ½ ounce camphor; cook the garlic in oil and strain and add the other ingredients. This will cure the worst case.

Whooping Cough, Asthma, and Worms

Garlic is recommended for whooping cough, colds, asthma, and worms. Horseradish is well known to cure hoarseness, dropsy, rheumatism, and palsy. The recipe is simple. Make a syrup by boiling the horseradish root, and adding sufficient sugar to make palatable. A dose is two or three teaspoonfuls two or three times a day.

In July, August, and September the root of the dandelion should be collected and a strong tea of infusion made, and drunk freely, two or three times daily for chronic biliousness, inflammation of the liver, constipation and coughs.

Tapeworm in Man or Horse

Take 4 ounces of powdered pumpkin seeds and a half pound of veal; cook together until substance is out of meat and made into a soup. The patient must fast for twenty-four hours, then eat half of the soup. After an hour eat the other half, then take a brisk cathartic. This is the proportion for a man. For a horse; one pound of pumpkin seeds to one pound of veal. It is given as a drench. This remedy is easily obtained and gives decided relief.

Skin Diseases

The American Indian knew the many uses of juniper berries long before Columbus landed on these shores. The early pioneers learned the formulas and recipes for native plants and herbs from the red man. One of the ever ready trees found useful is the juniper. Berries from this common Southwestern tree are often eaten for dropsy, skin diseases, and scrofula. They can be taken dry or fresh, but it is best if the berries are bruised by breaking with a hammer before taking.

Removal of Warts

Rub castor oil on warts for several weeks. In most cases they will drop off. Or touch warts daily with acetic acid. Warts can also be removed by small doses of sulphate of magnesia (epsom salts) taken internally, daily, for from 1 to 3 weeks; never use caustic potash or nitric acid.

Sand Bag Warmer

Get some clean, fine sand, dry it thoroughly in a pan on the stove. Make a bag about 8 inches square of flannel, fill it with the dry sand, sewing the opening carefully together, and cover the bag with cotton or linen cloth. This will prevent the sand from sifting out, and will also enable you to heat the bag quickly by placing in the oven. After once using this no one will ever attempt to warm the hands or feet of a sick person with a bottle of hot water or a brick. The sand holds the heat a long time, and the bag can be tucked up to the back without hurting one. It is a good plan to make 2 or 3 of these bags and keep them ready for use. Children with toothache or earache can be put to sleep many a time with a sand bag.

— From *Queen of the Household*

Index